SPECTRUM®

Geometry

Grades 6–8

Published by Spectrum®
an imprint of Carson Dellosa Education
Greensboro, NC

Spectrum®
An imprint of Carson Dellosa Education
P.O. Box 35665
Greensboro, NC 27425 USA

Printed in the USA • All rights reserved.   ISBN 978-1-4838-1662-3

02-174207784

Table of Contents Geometry

Table of Contents, continued

Check What You Know

Points, Lines, Rays, and Angles

1. Under each of the following items, write *line*, *line segment*, or *ray*. Then, circle the correct names. Each has more than one correct name.

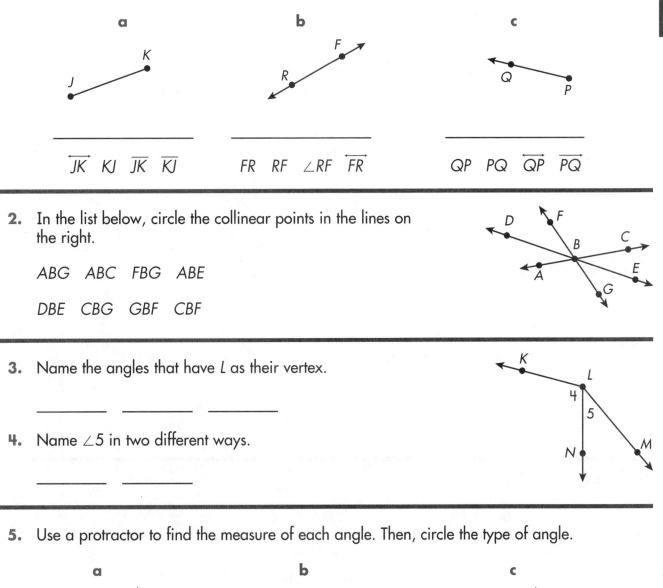

a

_____

$\overrightarrow{JK}$ KJ $\overline{JK}$ $\overline{KJ}$

b

_____

FR RF $\angle RF$ $\overleftrightarrow{FR}$

c

_____

QP PQ $\overleftrightarrow{QP}$ $\overline{PQ}$

2. In the list below, circle the collinear points in the lines on the right.

ABG   ABC   FBG   ABE

DBE   CBG   GBF   CBF

3. Name the angles that have *L* as their vertex.

_____   _____   _____

4. Name ∠5 in two different ways.

_____   _____

5. Use a protractor to find the measure of each angle. Then, circle the type of angle.

a

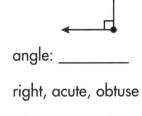

angle: _____

right, acute, obtuse

b

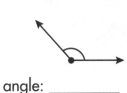

angle: _____

right, acute, obtuse

c

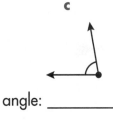

angle: _____

right, acute, obtuse

Lesson 1.1　Points and Lines

A **point** has no dimensions but defines a location in space.

Point *R* is shown at right.

A **line** extends infinitely in both directions.

Line *ST* is the same as line *TS* and can also be named $\overleftrightarrow{ST}$ or $\overleftrightarrow{TS}$.

A **line segment** is the part of the line between two **end points**.

Segment *UV* is the same as segment *VU* and can also be named $\overline{UV}$ or $\overline{VU}$.

Name the following figures. The first answer is given.

		a	b
1.	 *A*　*B*	line *AB* or *BA*	$\overrightarrow{AB}$ or $\overrightarrow{BA}$
2.	 *C*　*D*	line ____ or ____	_____ or _____
3.	 *E*　*F*	line ____ or ____	_____ or _____

		a	b	c
4.	 *G*　*H*	line segment *GH* or ____	$\overline{GH}$ or ____	endpoints ____ and ____
5.	 *J*　*K*	line segment *JK* or ____	$\overline{JK}$ or ____	endpoints ____ and ____

Draw the following figures.

	a	b
6.	line *LM*	$\overleftrightarrow{PQ}$
7.	$\overline{RS}$	$\overleftrightarrow{TU}$

Lesson 1.1   Points and Lines

Collinear points are three or more points on the same straight line.

Points that do not appear on the same straight line are **noncollinear**.

A **midpoint** is the point halfway between the end points on a line segment.
On the line *WY* at right, the midpoint is *X*.

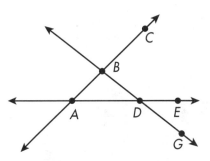

1. In the list below, circle the collinear points in the lines on
    the right. (There is more than one correct answer.)

    MKL

    MKJ

    MKN

    JKL

2. In the list below, circle the collinear points in the lines on
    the right. (There is more than one correct answer.)

    ABC

    BDG

    ABD

    DBC

    EDG

    ADE

3. In the list below, circle the correct names for the item on the right.

    $\overrightarrow{LM}$ *ML* $\overleftrightarrow{ML}$ *LM*

4. Draw a line segment using the points on the right, and then name it in the space below.

    N
    •

    O
    •

    _____

Lesson 1.2 Rays and Angles

A **ray** is a part of a line. It has one endpoint but extends infinitely in one direction. See ray *WX* or *WX*. It is *not* ray *XW*.

See angle *YWX*. An **angle** is the union of two rays that share a common endpoint. The two rays that make up the angle are called the **sides**. The endpoint (*W*) is called a **vertex**.

See angle *YWX*. It is the union of *WX* and *WY*. Angle *YWX* can be written as ∠*XWY*, ∠*YWX*, or ∠*W*. The vertex (∠*W*) stands for the angle.

At right is an angle formed by the union of *CA* and *CE*. It can be written as ∠*ACE*, ∠*ECA*, or ∠*C*. It could also be called angle 4.

Complete the following. The first answer is given.

	a		**b**

1. ray *CD* $\overrightarrow{CD}$ endpoint *C*

2. ray _____ _____   endpoint _____

3. ray _____ _____   endpoint _____

Name each figure using letters. Name each figure in more than one way, if you can.

4. _____

5. _____

Lesson 1.3 Measuring Angles

Use a protractor to measure angles. Place the center point of the protractor on the vertex of the angle you want to measure.

The measure of a **right angle** is 90°.

The measure of an **acute angle** is less than 90°.

The measure of an **obtuse angle** is greater than 90°.

The measure of ∠XYZ is 50°.

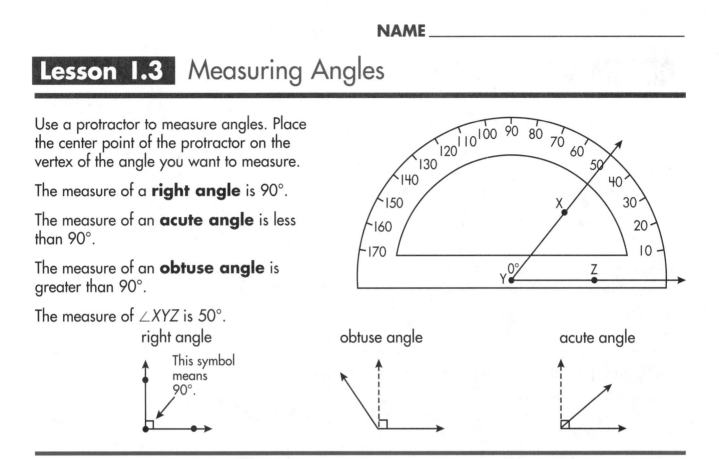

right angle

This symbol means 90°.

obtuse angle

acute angle

Find the measure of each angle. Write whether the angle is *right*, *acute*, or *obtuse*.

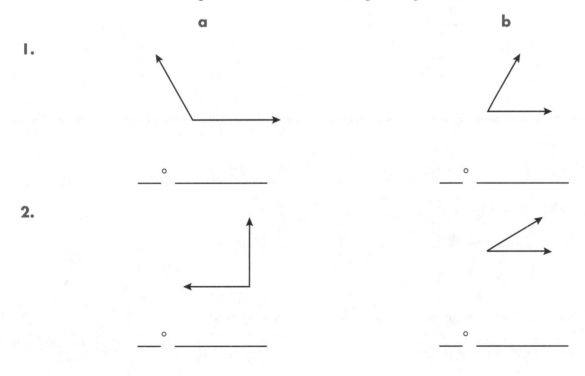

a   b

1.

____° _____   ____° _____

2.

____° _____   ____° _____

Lesson 1.4   Angle Relationships

When two lines intersect, they form angles that have special relationships.

Vertical angles are opposite angles that have the same measure.

Supplementary angles are two angles whose measures have a sum of 180°.

Complementary angles are two angles whose measures have a sum of 90°.

A **bisector** divides an angle into two angles of equal measure.

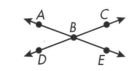

∠ABC and ∠DBE are vertical.

∠ABD and ∠DBE are supplementary.

∠WXZ and ∠ZXY are complementary.

$\overrightarrow{XZ}$ is the bisector of ∠WXY.

Identify each pair of angles as *supplementary* or *vertical*.

1. ∠AGB and ∠HGE _____

2. ∠BGE and ∠HGE _____

3. ∠GEC and ∠CED _____

4. ∠GEC and ∠DEF _____

5. ∠AGH and ∠BGE _____

6. ∠GEF and ∠DEF _____

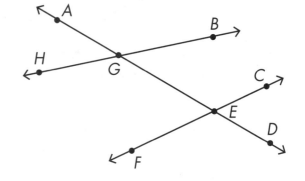

Solve each problem.

7. ∠A and ∠G are vertical angles. The measure of ∠A is 72°.

   What is the measure of ∠G? _____

8. ∠Y and ∠Z are supplementary angles. The measure of ∠Y is 112°.

   What is the measure of ∠Z? _____

9. ∠A and ∠B are complementary angles. The measure of ∠A is 53°.

   What is the measure of ∠B? _____

10. ∠RST is bisected by ray SW. The measure of ∠WST is 30°.

    What is the measure of ∠RST? _____

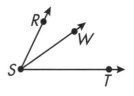

Lesson 1.5 Transversals

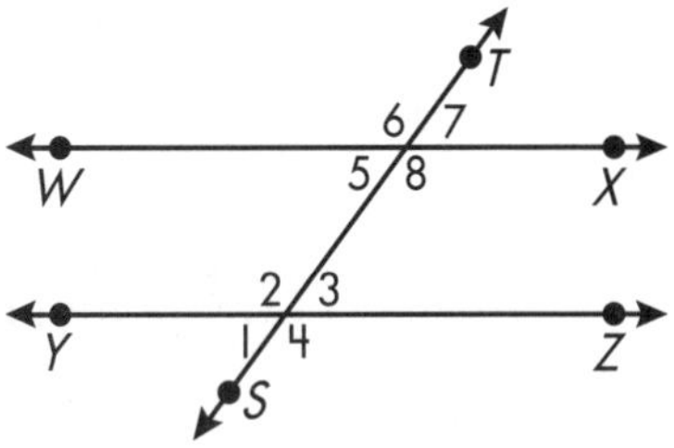

Parallel lines are two lines that will never meet. In the figure, $\overleftrightarrow{WX}$ and $\overleftrightarrow{YZ}$ are parallel lines.

A **transversal** is a line that intersects two parallel lines. $\overleftrightarrow{ST}$ is a transversal of $\overleftrightarrow{YZ}$ and $\overleftrightarrow{WX}$.

Corresponding angles are formed when a transversal intersects parallel lines. Corresponding angles are angles $\angle 1$ and $\angle 5$, $\angle 2$ and $\angle 6$, $\angle 3$ and $\angle 7$, and $\angle 4$ and $\angle 8$.

Adjacent angles are any two angles that are next to one another, such as $\angle 1/\angle 2$ and $\angle 2/\angle 3$. Adjacent angles share a ray. They form supplementary angles (180°).

1. Name the pairs of adjacent angles in the figure.

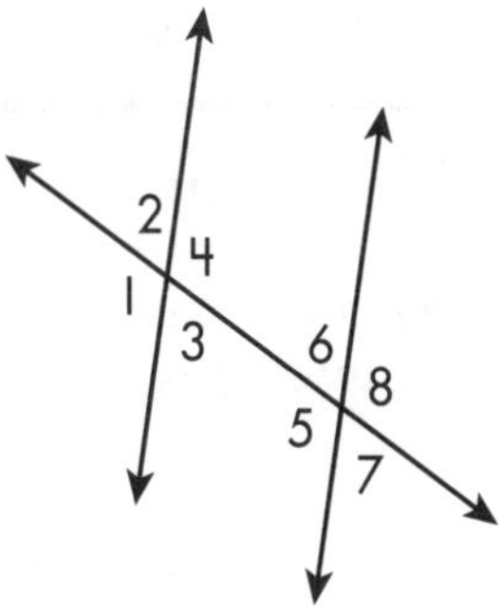

   $\angle$___/$\angle$___, $\angle$___/$\angle$___, $\angle$___/$\angle$___, $\angle$___/$\angle$___,

   $\angle$___/$\angle$___, $\angle$___/$\angle$___, $\angle$___/$\angle$___, $\angle$___/$\angle$___,

Alternate interior angles are those that are inside the parallel lines and opposite one another. $\angle 3$ and $\angle 6$ are alternate interior angles. They are congruent.

2. Name another pair of alternate interior angles in the figure. $\angle$_____/$\angle$_____

Alternate exterior angles are those that are outside the parallel lines and opposite one another. $\angle 1$ and $\angle 8$ are alternate exterior angles. They are congruent.

3. Name another pair of alternate exterior angles in the figure. $\angle$_____/$\angle$_____

List the following pairs of angles in the figure.

4. Adjacent:

   $\angle$___/$\angle$___, $\angle$___/$\angle$___, $\angle$___/$\angle$___, $\angle$___/$\angle$___,

   $\angle$___/$\angle$___, $\angle$___/$\angle$___, $\angle$___/$\angle$___, $\angle$___/$\angle$___,

5. Alternate interior: $\angle$_____/$\angle$_____, $\angle$_____/$\angle$_____

6. Alternate exterior: $\angle$_____/$\angle$_____, $\angle$_____/$\angle$_____

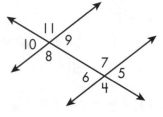

Check What You Learned

Points, Lines, Rays, and Angles

Use the figure to answer the following.

1. Name an angle that is vertical to ∠BJC. _____

2. Name an angle that is vertical to ∠ACG. _____

3. Name an angle that is supplementary to ∠JCD. _____

4. ∠DCJ is 90°. $\overrightarrow{CE}$ bisects ∠DCJ.
What is the angle measure of ∠DCE? _____

5. Name an angle that is complementary to ∠DCE. _____

Use the figure to answer the following.

6. Name the alternate interior angles.

∠_____/∠_____   ∠_____/∠_____

7. Name the alternate exterior angles.

∠_____/∠_____   ∠_____/∠_____

8. Assume ∠8 is 40°. What is the measure of ∠1? _____

Use the figure to answer the following.

9. Name the transversal of $\overleftrightarrow{AC}$ and $\overleftrightarrow{DF}$.

_____

∠1 and ∠4 are adjacent angles. They are supplementary.

10 If ∠4 is 150°, what is the measure of ∠1? _____

11. If ∠4 is 150°, what is the measure of ∠DEH? _____

Check What You Know

Triangle Properties and Relationships

Identify the square root of each perfect square.

a	b	c

1. $\sqrt{225}$ = _____ $\sqrt{64}$ = _____ $\sqrt{484}$ = _____

Estimate the following square roots. Example: $\sqrt{37}$ is between 6 and 7 but closer to 6.

2. $\sqrt{66}$ is between _____ and _____ but closer to _____.

3. $\sqrt{19}$ is between _____ and _____ but closer to _____.

Use the Pythagorean Theorem to determine the length of a, b, or c.

4. If $a = 36$ and $b = 48$, $c = \sqrt{}$ _____ or _____.

5. If $a = 98$ and $c = 170$, $b = \sqrt{}$ _____ or _____.

6. If $b = 77$ and $c = 122$, $a = \sqrt{}$ _____ or _____.

Solve.

7. Campers attached a rope to a pole 12 ft. high. They pulled it tight and staked it to the ground 16 ft. from the pole.

How long is the rope? _____

Find the lengths of the missing sides for the similar right triangles.

a	b	c

8. $AB =$ _____ m $DF =$ _____ m $EF =$ _____ m

Lesson 2.1 Triangles (by angles)

The sum of all angles in a triangle is always 180°.

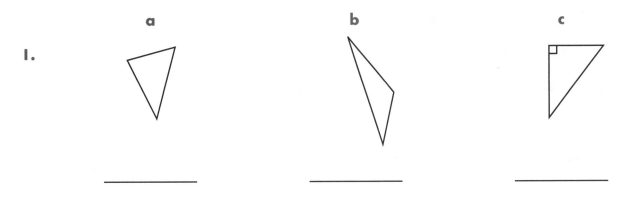

$52° + 38° + 90° = 180°$ $60° + 60° + 60° = 180°$ $33° + 120° + 27° = 180°$

A **right triangle** contains 1 right angle, an angle of exactly 90°. Triangle A is a right triangle.

An **acute triangle** contains only acute angles, angles that are less than 90°. Triangle B is an acute triangle.

An **obtuse triangle** contains 1 obtuse angle, an angle greater than 90°. Triangle C is an obtuse triangle.

Label each triangle as *acute*, *right*, or *obtuse*. Check the angles with a protractor, if necessary.

a   **b**   **c**

1.

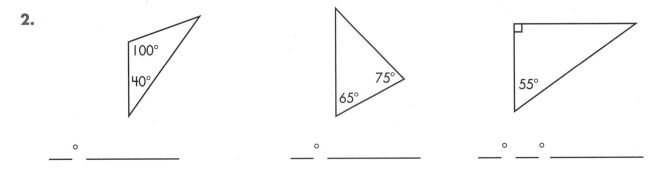

_____   _____   _____

Calculate the missing angle measures. Indicate whether the triangle is *acute*, *right*, or *obtuse*.

2.

___° _____ _____   ___° _____   ___° ___° _____

Lesson 2.2 Triangles (by sides)

Triangles can be classified by the number of congruent (equal) sides that they have.

In an **equilateral triangle**, all three sides are congruent.

In an **isosceles triangle**, at least two sides are congruent.

In a **scalene triangle**, no two sides are congruent.

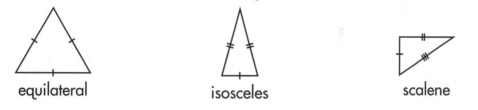

equilateral   isosceles   scalene

Use a ruler to measure each triangle. Write whether it is *equilateral*, *isosceles*, or *scalene*.

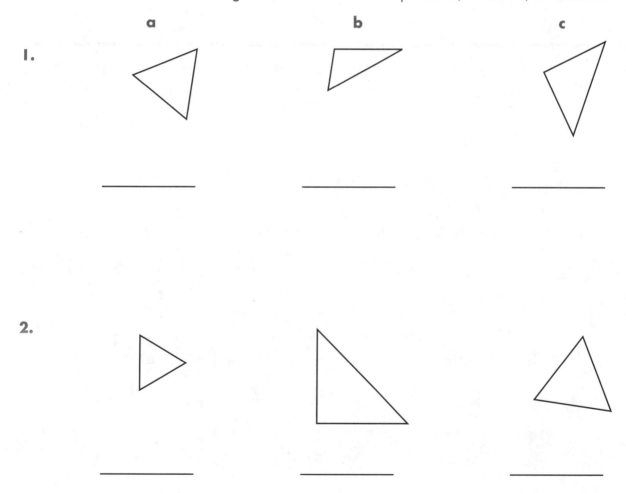

Lesson 2.3 Drawing Geometric Shapes: Triangles

When given two angle measures and one side length, a protractor and ruler can be used to create a triangle.

Draw a triangle that has angles of 30° and 80° and a side between them of two inches.

Step 1: Use a ruler to draw a line that is 2 inches.

Step 2: Use a protractor to draw a line that creates the desired angle with the first line (30°).

Step 3: Use the protractor to measure the 2nd known angle from the other end of your original line.

Step 4: Label the triangle.

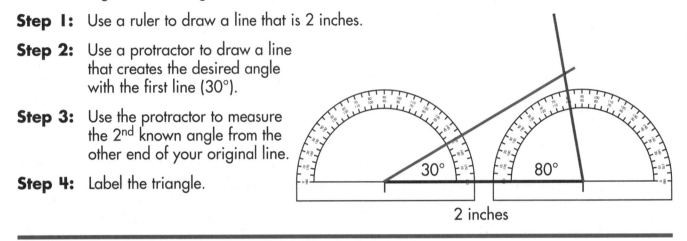

2 inches

Use the angles and side lengths given to create triangles. Label the measurements on your drawing.

	a	**b**
1.	angles: 50° and 55° side: 1 inch	angles: 120° and 30° side: 2 cm
2.	angles: 75° and 40° side: 3 inches	angles: 60° and 100° side: 2 inches

Lesson 2.3 Drawing Geometric Shapes: Triangles

When given the length of two sides and the measure of an angle that is not between the sides, a triangle can be drawn.

Draw a triangle that has sides of 2 inches and $1\frac{1}{2}$ inches and a non-included angle of 45°.

Step 1: Draw a line of any length.

Step 2: Use a protractor to draw a 2-inch line that creates the desired angle with the first line (45°).

Step 3: Use a compass set at $1\frac{1}{2}$ inches to find where the third line will intersect the base.

Step 4: Label the triangle.

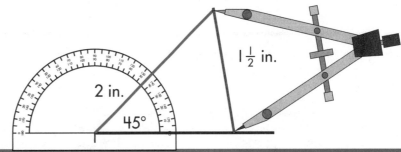

Use the angles and side lengths given to create triangles. Label the measurements on your drawing.

	a	b
1.	angle: 50° sides: 1 inch and 2 inches	angle: 140° sides: 3 cm and 4 cm
2.	angle: 85° sides: 2 inches and 4 inches	angle: 100° sides: 2 cm and 5 cm

Lesson 2.3 Drawing Geometric Shapes: Triangles

When given the lengths of three line segments, determine if the segments make a triangle by examining their relationship. Each pair of sides added together must be greater than the remaining side.

$a + b > c$

$a + c > b$

$b + c > a$

$4 + 2 > 3$

$4 + 3 > 2$

$3 + 2 > 4$

Because the measurements follow the rules, the side lengths make a triangle.

Using the given lengths, determine if they will make a triangle. Circle *yes* or *no*.

	a	**b**	**c**

1.

a: Side 1: 5 inches / Side 2: 3 inches / Side 3: 2 inches

yes   no

b: Side 1: 3 feet / Side 2: 8 feet / Side 3: 7 feet

yes   no

c: Side 1: 10 inches / Side 2: 4 inches / Side 3: 12 inches

yes   no

2.

a: Side 1: 5 centimeters / Side 2: 8 centimeters / Side 3: 20 centimeters

yes   no

b: Side 1: 5 meters / Side 2: 9 meters / Side 3: 20 meters

yes   no

c: Side 1: 10 inches / Side 2: 10 inches / Side 3: 19 inches

yes   no

3.

a: Side 1: 4 millimeters / Side 2: 9 millimeters / Side 3: 9 millimeters

yes   no

b: Side 1: 4 inches / Side 2: 4 inches / Side 3: 7 inches

yes   no

c: Side 1: 7 centimeters / Side 2: 5 centimeters / Side 3: 14 centimeters

yes   no

4.

a: Side 1: 3 centimeters / Side 2: 3 centimeters / Side 3: 10 centimeters

yes   no

b: Side 1: 4 yards / Side 2: 8 yards / Side 3: 6 yards

yes   no

c: Side 1: 2 meters / Side 2: 3 meters / Side 3: 4 meters

yes   no

Lesson 2.4 Similar Triangles

Two triangles are **similar** if their corresponding (matching) angles are congruent (have the same measure) and the lengths of their corresponding sides are proportional.

The triangles on the right are similar.

All the sides are proportional:

$$\frac{AB}{DE} = \frac{12}{8} = \frac{3}{2} \qquad \frac{BC}{EF} = \frac{12}{8} = \frac{3}{2} \qquad \frac{AC}{DF} = \frac{9}{6} = \frac{3}{2}$$

The angle measures are congruent.

The lower triangles on the right are not similar. The sides are not proportional. They do not all create the same ratio.

The angle measures are not all congruent.

$$\frac{GH}{JK} = \frac{4}{3} \qquad \frac{HI}{KL} = \frac{6}{5} \qquad \frac{GI}{JL} = \frac{5}{5} = \frac{1}{1}$$

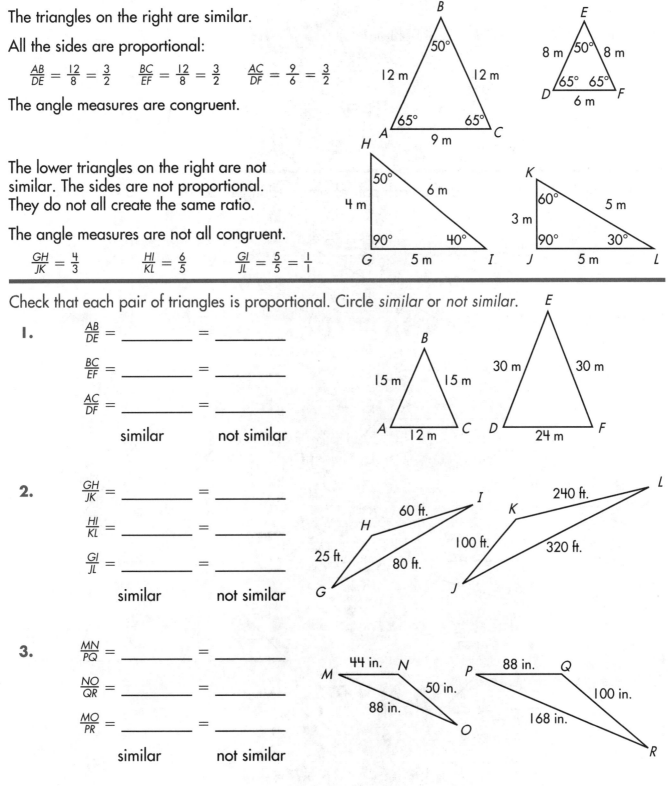

Check that each pair of triangles is proportional. Circle *similar* or *not similar*.

1. $\frac{AB}{DE} =$ _____ = _____

$\frac{BC}{EF} =$ _____ = _____

$\frac{AC}{DF} =$ _____ = _____

similar   not similar

2. $\frac{GH}{JK} =$ _____ = _____

$\frac{HI}{KL} =$ _____ = _____

$\frac{GI}{JL} =$ _____ = _____

similar   not similar

3. $\frac{MN}{PQ} =$ _____ = _____

$\frac{NO}{QR} =$ _____ = _____

$\frac{MO}{PR} =$ _____ = _____

similar   not similar

Lesson 2.4 Similar Triangles

When you know that two triangles are similar,
you can use the ratio of the known lengths
of the sides to figure the unknown length.

For example, assume the triangles at right are
similar. What is the length of *EF*? Use a proportion.

$\frac{AC}{DF} = \frac{BC}{EF}$ $\frac{4}{6} = \frac{12}{n}$ Cross multiply.
$$4n = 72 \quad n = 18$$

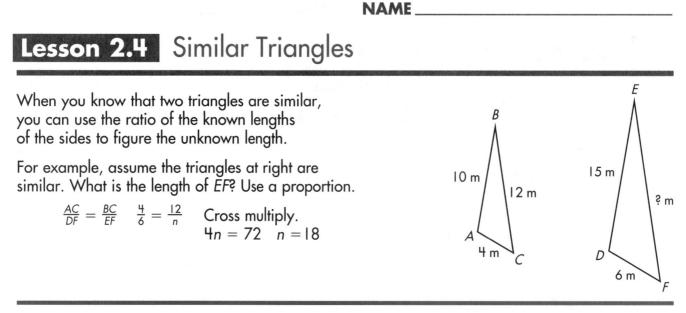

Find the length of the missing side for each pair of similar triangles. Label the side with its length.

a b

1.

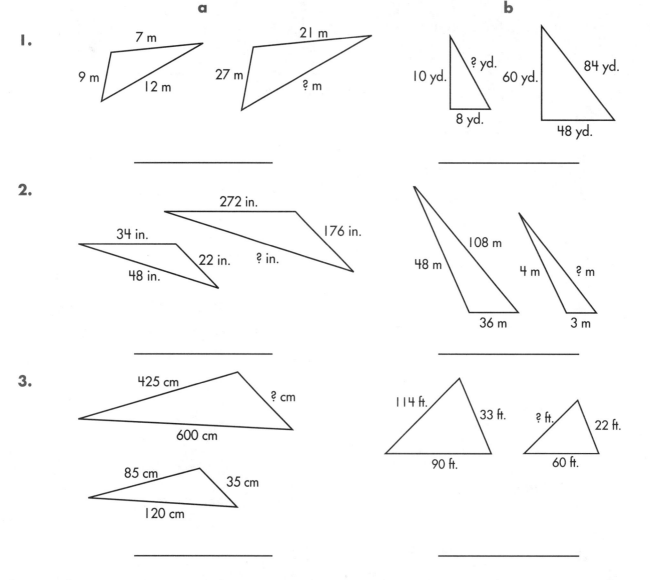

7 m   21 m
9 m   12 m   27 m   ? m

? yd.   84 yd.
10 yd.   60 yd.
8 yd.   48 yd.

_____   _____

2.

272 in.
34 in.   176 in.
22 in.   ? in.
48 in.

108 m
48 m   4 m   ? m
36 m   3 m

_____   _____

3.

425 cm   ? cm
600 cm

114 ft.   33 ft.   ? ft.   22 ft.
90 ft.   60 ft.

85 cm   35 cm
120 cm

_____   _____

Lesson 2.5 Ratio and Proportion

A **ratio** is a comparison of 2 numbers. A ratio can be expressed as 1 to 2, 1:2, or $\frac{1}{2}$. In this example, the ratio means that for every 1 of the first item, there are 2 of the other item.

A **proportion** expresses the equality of 2 ratios. Cross-multiply to determine if two ratios are equal.

$\frac{4}{2} \bowtie \frac{2}{1}$ $4 \times 1 = 2 \times 2$, so the proportion is true.

$\frac{3}{4} = \frac{2}{3}$ $3 \times 3 \neq 4 \times 2$, so the proportion is **not** true.

Cross-multiply to check each proportion. Show your work. Write *T* next to proportions that are true.

	a	**b**	**c**
1.	$\frac{1}{2} = \frac{3}{6}$ _____	$\frac{5}{8} = \frac{3}{10}$ _____	$\frac{1}{3} = \frac{3}{9}$ _____
2.	$4:9 = 9:4$ _____	$\frac{3}{18} = \frac{1}{6}$ _____	2 to 5 = 5 to 12 _____
3.	$\frac{1}{4} = \frac{11}{44}$ _____	6 to 3 = 7 to 6 _____	$\frac{6}{7} = \frac{18}{21}$ _____
4.	$\frac{3}{2} = 6:3$ _____	4 to 3 = 20:15 _____	$\frac{4}{3} = \frac{16}{9}$ _____
5.	$10:12 = \frac{30}{36}$ _____	$\frac{3}{8} = \frac{9}{24}$ _____	$\frac{13}{26} = \frac{1}{2}$ _____
6.	$\frac{3}{4} = \frac{9}{14}$ _____	$5:3 = \frac{11}{7}$ _____	$\frac{3}{6} = \frac{8}{4}$ _____
7.	$\frac{7}{5} = \frac{35}{25}$ _____	$3:16 = 9:48$ _____	$\frac{9}{6} = \frac{14}{8}$ _____

Lesson 2.6 Solving Proportion Equations

You can use a proportion to solve problems.

The ratio of apples to oranges in a basket is 4 to 5. There are 20 oranges in the basket. How many apples are there?

$\frac{4}{5} = \frac{n}{20}$ Set up a proportion, using n for the missing number.

$4 \times 20 = 5 \times n$ Cross-multiply.

$\frac{80}{5} = n$ Solve for n.

$16 = n$ There are 16 apples.

The missing number can appear anyplace in a proportion. Solve the same way.

$\frac{2}{3} = \frac{6}{n}$ $\frac{n}{4} = \frac{3}{6}$

$3 \times 6 = 2 \times n$ $4 \times 3 = 6 \times n$

$\frac{18}{2} = n$ $\frac{12}{6} = n$

$9 = n$ $2 = n$

Solve for n in each proportion.

	a	b	c
1.	$\frac{3}{4} = \frac{n}{16}$ _____	$3:5 = n:20$ _____	$\frac{1}{7} = \frac{9}{n}$ _____
2.	$\frac{n}{8} = \frac{5}{2}$ _____	$18:n = 6:3$ _____	2 to $6 = 20$ to n _____
3.	$\frac{n}{11} = \frac{5}{55}$ _____	$\frac{6}{n} = \frac{20}{10}$ _____	$n:18 = 3:27$ _____

Write a proportion for each problem. Then, solve the problem.

4. Emilio wants to make a pumpkin pie for each of his 5 cousins. One pie requires 15 ounces of pumpkin filling. How many ounces of filling must Emilio buy?

_____ Emilio must buy _____ ounces of filling.

5. Julia owns a home worth $100,000. She must pay $5 in property tax for every $1,000 of her home's value. How much property tax will Julia pay?

_____ Julia will pay _____ in property tax.

Lesson 2.7 Proportions and Scale Drawings

A **scale drawing** is a drawing of a real object in which all of the dimensions are proportional to the real object. A scale drawing can be larger or smaller than the object it represents. The **scale** is the ratio of the drawing size to the actual size of the object.

A drawing of a person has a scale of 2 inches = 1 foot. If the drawing is 11 inches high, how tall is the person?

$$\frac{2}{1} = \frac{11}{n}$$ Write a proportion.

$1 \times 11 = n \times 2$ Solve for n.

$5\frac{1}{2} = n$ The person is $5\frac{1}{2}$ feet tall.

Write a proportion for each problem. Then, solve the problem.

1. A map of Ohio uses a scale of 1 inch = 11 miles. The map is 20 inches wide. How wide is Ohio?

    _____ Ohio is _____ miles wide.

2. The Statue of Liberty is 305 feet tall. A scale drawing has a ratio of 1 inch = 5 feet. How tall is the drawing?

    _____ The drawing is _____ inches tall.

3. A customer asked Lan's Photo Shop to enlarge a photograph to make a poster 24 inches long. The original photo is 6 inches long. How many inches will the shop enlarge the photo for every inch of the original length?

    _____ The enlargement will be _____ inches for every inch.

4. A landscape designer made a scale drawing of a client's yard. The scale is 2 inches to 5 feet. The yard is 70 feet wide. How wide is the drawing?

    _____ The drawing is _____ inches wide.

5. A coach uses a scale drawing of a soccer field to design plays. The drawing is 27.5 centimeters long. The scale is 1 centimeter to 4 meters. How long is the soccer field?

    _____ The soccer field is _____ meters long.

Lesson 2.8 Problem Solving

Solve each problem. Write a proportion in the space to the right.

1. A bridge is 440 yards long. A scale drawing has a ratio of 1 inch = 1 yard. How long is the drawing?

   The drawing is _____ inches long.

   1.

2. A map of the county uses a scale of 2 inches = 19 miles. If the county is 76 miles wide, how wide is the map?

   The map is _____ inches wide.

   2.

3. A picture of a fish has a scale of 8 centimeters to 3 centimeters. If the actual fish is 12 centimeters long, how long is the drawing?

   The drawing is _____ centimeters long.

   3.

4. An architect made a scale drawing of a house to be built. The scale is 2 inches to 3 feet. The house in the drawing is 24 inches tall. How tall is the actual house?

   The actual house is _____ feet tall.

   4.

5. A drawing of a new car uses a scale of 4 inches = 5 feet. The drawing of the car is 10 inches long. How long is the car?

   The car is _____ feet long.

   5.

6. A figurine of a famous person uses a scale of 1 inch = 8 inches. The person is 5 feet 4 inches, or 64 inches, tall. How tall is the figurine?

   The figurine is _____ inches tall.

   6.

Lesson 2.8 Problem Solving

Solve each problem. Write a proportion in the space to the right.

1. On an architect's blueprint, the front of a building measures 27 inches wide. The scale of the blueprint is 1 inch = 2 feet. How wide will the front of the actual building be?

   The building will be _____ feet wide.

   1.

2. The model of an airplane has a wingspan of 20 inches. The model has a scale of 1 inch = 4 feet. What is the wingspan of the actual airplane?

   The wingspan is _____ feet.

   2.

3. A picture of a car uses a scale of 1 inch = $\frac{1}{2}$ foot. The actual car is $8\frac{1}{2}$ feet wide. How wide will the drawing of the car be?

   The drawing will be _____ inches wide.

   3.

4. On a map, two cities are $4\frac{1}{2}$ inches apart. The scale of the map is $\frac{1}{2}$ inch = 3 miles. What is the actual distance between the cities?

   The actual distance is _____ miles.

   4.

5. Marisa is making a scale drawing of her house. Her house is 49 feet wide. On her drawing, the house is 7 inches wide. What is the scale of Marisa's drawing?

   The scale is _____.

   5.

6. The bed of Jeff's pick-up truck is 8 feet long. On a scale model of his truck, the bed is 10 inches long. What is the scale of the model?

   The scale is _____.

   6.

Lesson 2.9 Squares and Square Roots

The **square** of a number is that number multiplied by itself. A square is expressed as 6^2, which means 6×6 or *6 squared*. The **square root** of a number is the number that, multiplied by itself, equals that number. The square root of 36 is 6: $\sqrt{36} = 6$.

Not all square roots of numbers are whole numbers like 6. Numbers that have a whole number as their square root are called **perfect squares**.

The square root of any number that is not a perfect square is called a **radical number**. The symbol $\sqrt{}$ is called a **radical sign**. When a number is not a perfect square, you can estimate its square root by determining which perfect squares it comes between.

$\sqrt{50}$ is a little more than 7, because $\sqrt{49}$ is exactly 7. $\sqrt{60}$ is between 7 and 8 but closer to 8, because 60 is closer to 64 than to 49.

If you need help with squares or square roots, refer to the Table of Squares and Square Roots at the back of this book.

Identify the square root of each perfect square.

	a	b	c
1.	$\sqrt{9} =$ _____	$\sqrt{81} =$ _____	$\sqrt{49} =$ _____
2.	$\sqrt{4} =$ _____	$\sqrt{100} =$ _____	$\sqrt{144} =$ _____
3.	$\sqrt{225} =$ _____	$\sqrt{196} =$ _____	$\sqrt{324} =$ _____

Estimate the following square roots.

4. $\sqrt{8}$ is between _____ and _____ but closer to _____.

5. $\sqrt{80}$ is between _____ and _____ but closer to _____.

6. $\sqrt{140}$ is between _____ and _____ but closer to _____.

7. $\sqrt{88}$ is between _____ and _____ but closer to _____.

8. $\sqrt{250}$ is between _____ and _____ but closer to _____.

Lesson 2.10 The Pythagorean Theorem

The **Pythagorean Theorem** states that the square of the length of the hypotenuse of a right triangle is equal to the sum of the squares of the other two sides. This is true for all right triangles.

In a right triangle, the hypotenuse is the side opposite the right angle. The other two sides are called legs. In this figure, c is the hypotenuse and a and b are the legs.

If a, b, and c are the lengths of the sides of this triangle, $a^2 + b^2 = c^2$.

If $a = 3$ and $b = 4$, what is c?

$a^2 + b^2 = c^2$ $3^2 + 4^2 = c^2$ $9 + 16 = c^2$ $25 = c^2$ $\sqrt{25} = c^2$ $5 = c$

If $a = 4$ and $b = 6$, what is b?

$a^2 + b^2 = c^2$ $4^2 + 6^2 = c^2$ $16 + 36 = c^2$ $52 = c^2$ $\sqrt{52} = c^2$ $\sqrt{52} = c$, about 7.21

Use the Pythagorean Theorem to determine the length of c. Assume that each problem describes a right triangle. Sides a and b are the legs and the hypotenuse is c. If necessary, round your answer to the nearest hundredth.

1. If $a = 7$ and $b = 5$, $c = \sqrt{\underline{\hspace{2cm}}}$ or about _____.

2. If $a = 6$ and $b = 8$, $c = \sqrt{\underline{\hspace{2cm}}}$ or _____.

3. If $a = 9$ and $b = 4$, $c = \sqrt{\underline{\hspace{2cm}}}$ or about _____.

4. If $a = 3$ and $b = 5$, $c = \sqrt{\underline{\hspace{2cm}}}$ or about _____.

5. If $a = 2$ and $b = 6$, $c = \sqrt{\underline{\hspace{2cm}}}$ or about _____.

6. If $a = 6$ and $b = 9$, $c = \sqrt{\underline{\hspace{2cm}}}$ or about _____.

7. If $a = 4$ and $b = 8$, $c = \sqrt{\underline{\hspace{2cm}}}$ or about _____.

8. If $a = 3$ and $b = 4$, $c = \sqrt{\underline{\hspace{2cm}}}$ or _____.

9. If $a = 2$ and $b = 9$, $c = \sqrt{\underline{\hspace{2cm}}}$ or about _____.

10. If $a = 5$ and $b = 9$, $c = \sqrt{\underline{\hspace{2cm}}}$ or about _____.

Lesson 2.11 Proofs of the Pythagorean Theorem

There are many ways to prove the Pythagorean Theorem.

One way is to draw squares on each of the sides of a right triangle.

Let a right triangle have sides of length 3, 4, and 5. Draw squares on the three sides as shown in the diagram. Divide each square into smaller squares. Count the number of squares on the two shorter sides and the number of squares on the longest side. The sum of the squares on the two shorter sides equals the number of squares on the longest side, $4^2 + 3^2 = 5^2$, or $a^2 + b^2 = c^2$.

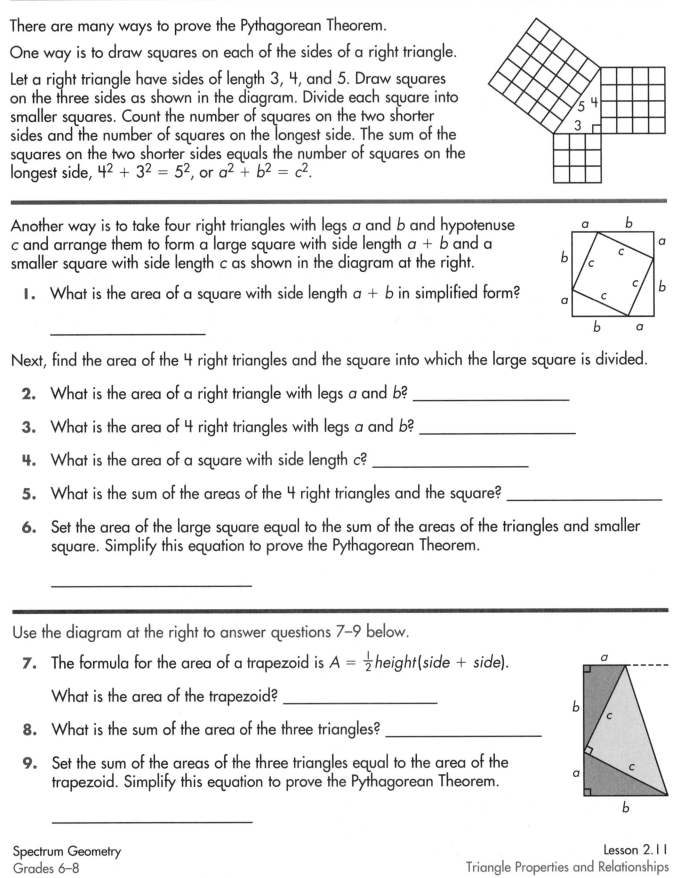

Another way is to take four right triangles with legs a and b and hypotenuse c and arrange them to form a large square with side length $a + b$ and a smaller square with side length c as shown in the diagram at the right.

1. What is the area of a square with side length $a + b$ in simplified form?

   _____

Next, find the area of the 4 right triangles and the square into which the large square is divided.

2. What is the area of a right triangle with legs a and b? _____

3. What is the area of 4 right triangles with legs a and b? _____

4. What is the area of a square with side length c? _____

5. What is the sum of the areas of the 4 right triangles and the square? _____

6. Set the area of the large square equal to the sum of the areas of the triangles and smaller square. Simplify this equation to prove the Pythagorean Theorem.

   _____

Use the diagram at the right to answer questions 7–9 below.

7. The formula for the area of a trapezoid is $A = \frac{1}{2} height(side + side)$.

   What is the area of the trapezoid? _____

8. What is the sum of the area of the three triangles? _____

9. Set the sum of the areas of the three triangles equal to the area of the trapezoid. Simplify this equation to prove the Pythagorean Theorem.

   _____

Lesson 2.11 Proofs of the Pythagorean Theorem

The Pythagorean Theorem is used to find the lengths of the sides of a right triangle. If you know the lengths of the sides of a triangle, and the sides satisfy the equation $a^2 + b^2 = c^2$, then the triangle must be a right triangle. This is called the converse of the Pythagorean Theorem.

Complete the questions below to prove the converse of the Pythagorean Theorem.

Given: Triangle I has side lengths a, b, and c such that $a^2 + b^2 = c^2$.

Triangle II is a right triangle with legs of side lengths a and b and a hypotenuse with side length d.

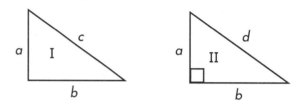

Prove: Triangle I is a right triangle.

1. Write an equation about triangle II using the Pythagorean Theorem.

_____

2. Write an equation for triangle I from the given information.

_____

3. Use the equations from questions 1 and 2 to compare c^2 and d^2.

_____

4. How do c and d compare?

_____

5. Why is triangle I congruent to triangle II?

_____

6. If triangle I is congruent to triangle II, what can you say about the measure of the angle across from the side of length c in triangle I?

_____

7. What type of triangle is triangle I?

_____

Lesson 2.12 The Pythagorean Theorem

Use the Pythagorean Theorem to find the unknown length of a side of a right triangle when the other two lengths are known.

If $a = 12$ m and $c = 13$ m, what is b?

$a^2 + b^2 = c^2$ $12^2 + b^2 = 13^2$

$144 + b^2 = 169$

$144 + b^2 - 144 = 169 - 144$

$b^2 = 25$ $b = \sqrt{25}$ $b = 5$ m

If $b = 15$ ft. and $c = 17$ ft., what is a?

$a^2 + b^2 = c^2$ $a^2 + 15^2 = 17^2$

$a^2 + 225 = 289$

$a^2 + 225 - 225 = 289 - 225$

$a^2 = 64$ $a = \sqrt{64}$ $a = 8$ ft.

Assume that each problem describes a right triangle. Use the Pythagorean Theorem to find the unknown lengths. If necessary, round your answer to the nearest hundredth.

1. If $a = 8$ and $c = 10$, $b = \sqrt{\rule{2cm}{0.4pt}}$ _____ or _____.

2. If $a = 12$ and $c = 16$, $b = \sqrt{\rule{2cm}{0.4pt}}$ _____ or _____.

3. If $b = 18$ and $c = 22$, $a = \sqrt{\rule{2cm}{0.4pt}}$ _____ or _____.

4. If $b = 8$ and $c = 14$, $a = \sqrt{\rule{2cm}{0.4pt}}$ _____ or _____.

5. If $a = 4$ and $c = 8$, $b = \sqrt{\rule{2cm}{0.4pt}}$ _____ or _____.

6. Alicia attached a support wire to the top of a flagpole. The wire was 65 ft. long, and she staked the wire 45 ft. from the pole. How tall was the flagpole?

The flagpole was _____ feet tall.

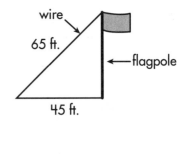

7. Tom is building a ramp to the back entrance of his house. The ramp will be attached to the house 12 ft. above the ground. He wants the end of the ramp to be 26 ft. from the house. What will be the length of the ramp?

The ramp will be _____ feet long.

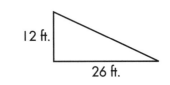

Lesson 2.13 Using the Pythagorean Theorem SHOW YOUR WORK

Use the Pythagorean Theorem to solve each problem.

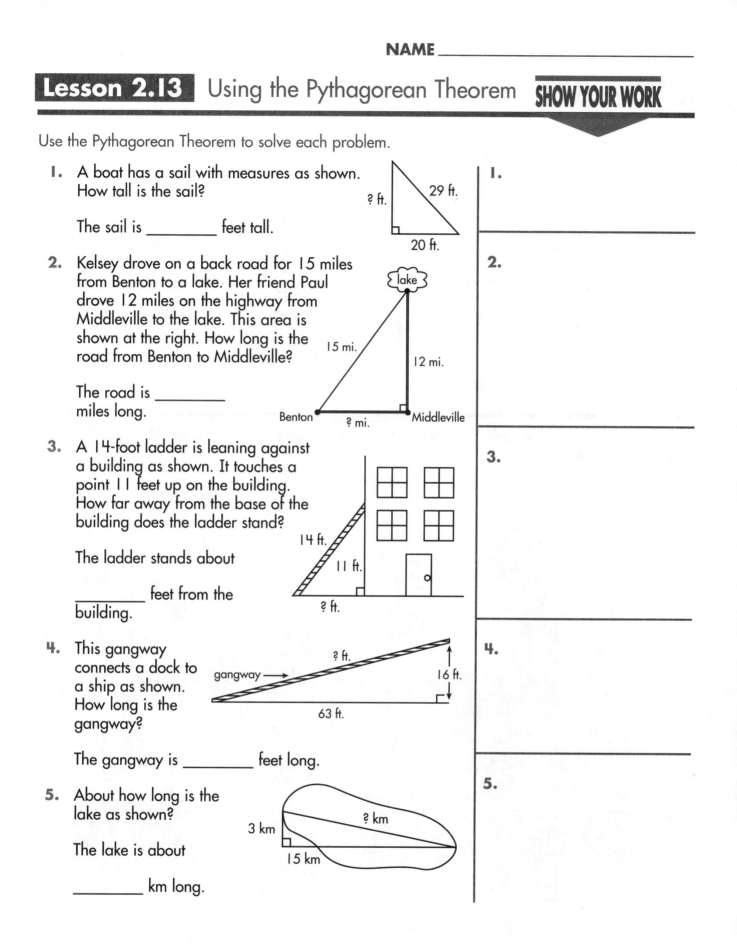

1. A boat has a sail with measures as shown. How tall is the sail?

   The sail is _____ feet tall.

2. Kelsey drove on a back road for 15 miles from Benton to a lake. Her friend Paul drove 12 miles on the highway from Middleville to the lake. This area is shown at the right. How long is the road from Benton to Middleville?

   The road is _____ miles long.

3. A 14-foot ladder is leaning against a building as shown. It touches a point 11 feet up on the building. How far away from the base of the building does the ladder stand?

   The ladder stands about

   _____ feet from the building.

4. This gangway connects a dock to a ship as shown. How long is the gangway?

   The gangway is _____ feet long.

5. About how long is the lake as shown?

   The lake is about

   _____ km long.

1.

2.

3.

4.

5.

Lesson 2.14 Pythagorean Theorem in the Coordinate Plane

The Pythagorean Theorem can be used to find an unknown distance between two points on a coordinate plane.

Find the distance between points A and B.

Step 1: Draw lines extending from points A and B so that when they intersect they create a right angle. Label the point at which they meet, point C.

Step 2: Find the distance of segment $\overline{AC}$ (7), and segment $\overline{BC}$ (6).

Step 3: Use Pythagorean Theorem to find the length of segment $\overline{AB}$.

$$7^2 + 6^2 = 85$$

$$(\overline{AB})^2 = 85$$

$$\overline{AB} = \sqrt{85} = 9.22$$

Find the distance between each of the points given below using the Pythagorean Theorem. Round to the nearest hundredth.

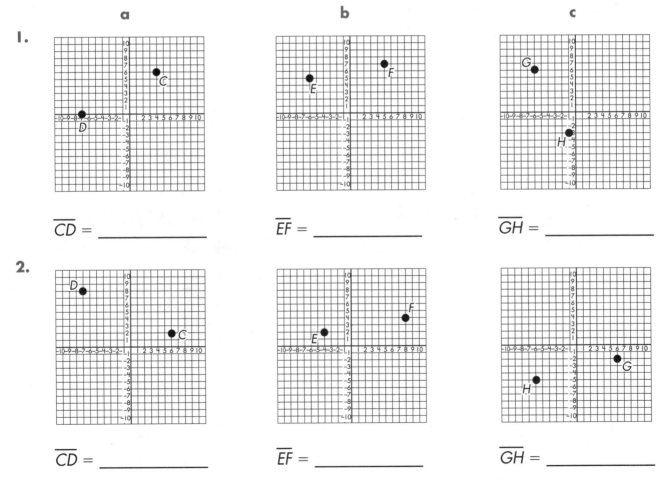

a	b	c
1.		
$\overline{CD} = $ _____	$\overline{EF} = $ _____	$\overline{GH} = $ _____
2.		
$\overline{CD} = $ _____	$\overline{EF} = $ _____	$\overline{GH} = $ _____

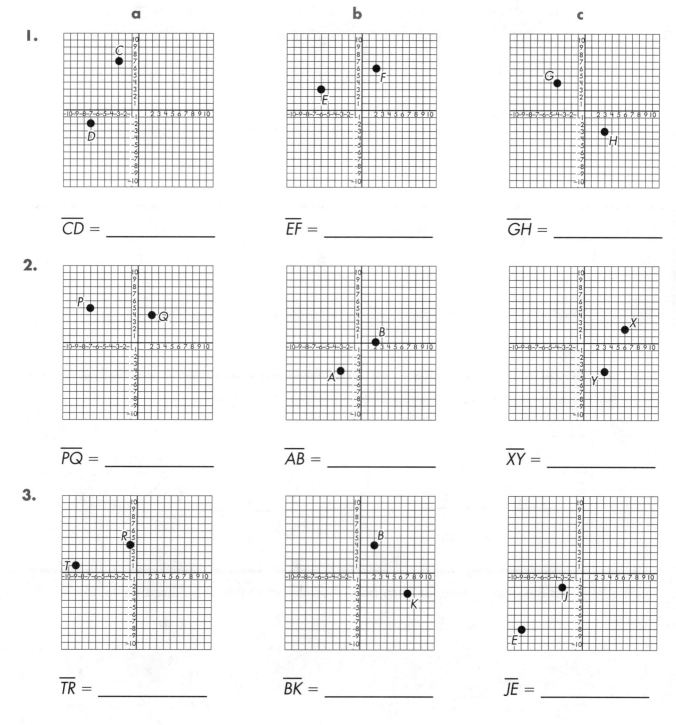

Lesson 2.14 Pythagorean Theorem in the Coordinate Plane

Find the distance between each of the points given below using the Pythagorean Theorem. Round to the nearest hundredth.

	a	b	c

1.

$\overline{CD} =$ _____ $\overline{EF} =$ _____ $\overline{GH} =$ _____

2.

$\overline{PQ} =$ _____ $\overline{AB} =$ _____ $\overline{XY} =$ _____

3.

$\overline{TR} =$ _____ $\overline{BK} =$ _____ $\overline{JE} =$ _____

Check What You Learned

Triangle Properties and Relationships

Calculate the missing angle measures. Indicate whether the triangle is *acute*, *right*, or *obtuse*.

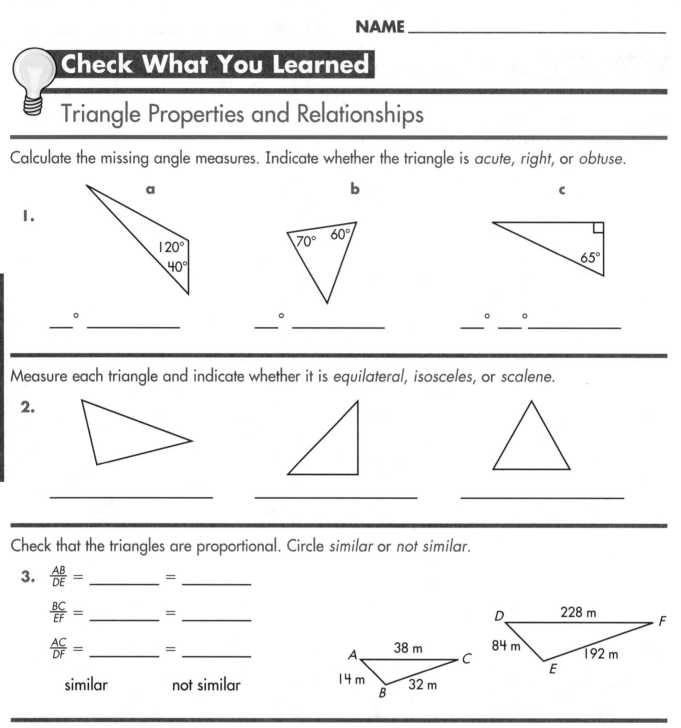

1.

    a   b   c

___° _____   ___° _____   ___° ___° _____

Measure each triangle and indicate whether it is *equilateral*, *isosceles*, or *scalene*.

2.

_____   _____   _____

Check that the triangles are proportional. Circle *similar* or *not similar*.

3. $\frac{AB}{DE} =$ _____ = _____

$\frac{BC}{EF} =$ _____ = _____

$\frac{AC}{DF} =$ _____ = _____

      similar   not similar

Find the length of the missing side for each pair of similar triangles. Label the side with its length.

4.

                    a   b

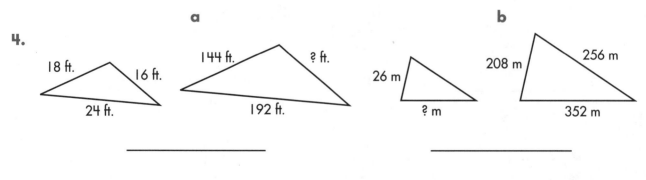

_____   _____

Check What You Learned

Triangle Properties and Relationships

Identify the square root of each perfect square.

a	b	c
5. $\sqrt{121} = $ _____	$\sqrt{256} = $ _____	$\sqrt{144} = $ _____

Estimate the square root.

6. $\sqrt{86}$ is between _____ and _____ but closer to _____.

Use the Pythagorean Theorem to determine the length of a, b, or c, rounding to the nearest hundredth.

7. If $a = 22$ and $b = 27$, $c = \sqrt{}$ or _____.

8. If $a = 48$ and $c = 92$, $b = \sqrt{}$ or _____.

9. If $b = 184$ and $c = 232$, $a = \sqrt{}$ or _____.

Solve.

10. Paul is building a deck within a corner of his house that measures 25 by 30 feet. How long will the deck extend from one corner of his house to the other, rounded to the nearest foot?

    The deck will be _____ feet.

Find the lengths of the missing sides for the similar right triangles.

a	b	c
11. $BC = $ _____ m	$DE = $ _____ m	$DF = $ _____ m

NAME _____

Check What You Know

Polygons

Write the name for each regular polygon. Find the sum of all of its angles and the measure of one angle.

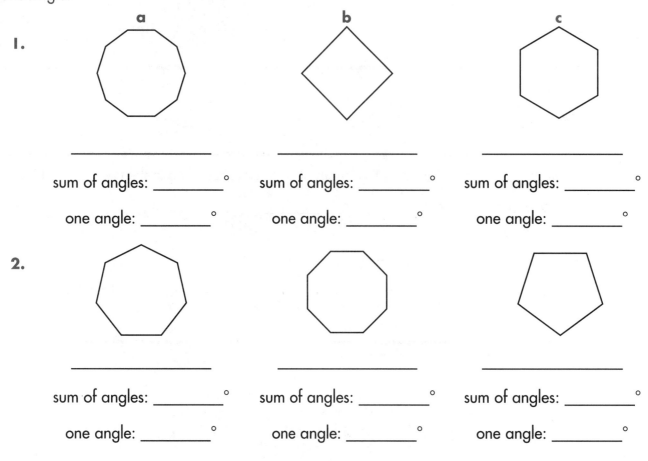

1.

    a   **b**   **c**

_____   _____   _____

sum of angles: _____°   sum of angles: _____°   sum of angles: _____°

one angle: _____°   one angle: _____°   one angle: _____°

2.

_____   _____   _____

sum of angles: _____°   sum of angles: _____°   sum of angles: _____°

one angle: _____°   one angle: _____°   one angle: _____°

Write the name for each polygon. Label it as *equiangular*, *equilateral*, or *regular*.

3.

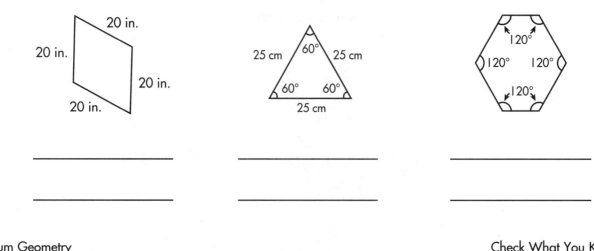

_____   _____   _____

_____   _____   _____

Lesson 3.1 Polygons

The **polygon** is a closed plane figure made up of straight lines. See the table at right. Polygons are named according to the number of their sides. A **triangle** has 3 sides and a **quadrilateral** has 4 sides.

If all the sides of a polygon are congruent (the same length), it is **equilateral**. If all its angles are congruent (the same measure), it is **equiangular**. If a polygon is both equilateral and equiangular, it is a **regular polygon**.

Prefix	Name	Sides
tri-	triangle	3
quadri-	quadrilateral	4
penta-	pentagon	5
hexa-	hexagon	6
hepta-	heptagon	7
octa-	octagon	8
nona-	nonagon	9
deca-	decagon	10

Find the sum of the measures of the interior angles of a polygon with the formula $(n - 2)180$ degrees, where n is the number of sides. To get the interior measure of one angle of the regular polygon, divide the sum by the number of sides. The following example is for a pentagon.

$(n - 2)180°$ $(5 - 2)180 = 540°$ $540° \div 5 = 108°$

Write the name for each regular polygon. Find the sum of all of its angles and the measure of one angle.

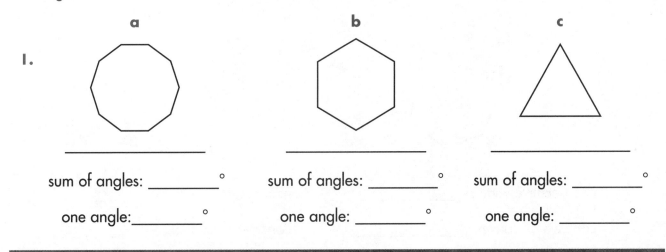

a   b   c

1.

_____   _____   _____

sum of angles: _____°   sum of angles: _____°   sum of angles: _____°

one angle: _____°   one angle: _____°   one angle: _____°

Name each polygon and label it as *equiangular*, *equilateral*, or *regular*.

2.

_____   _____   _____

_____   _____   _____

Lesson 3.1 Polygons

A **vertex** is the point where any two sides of a polygon meet. In figure A, the sides *AB* and *BC* meet at the vertex *B*. Since the sides *AB* and *BC* share a vertex, they are **consecutive sides**.

The two endpoints of a side, such as vertex *B* and vertex *C*, are called **consecutive vertices**. The dashed lines in figure A are diagonals. A **diagonal** is a line segment drawn between any two **nonconsecutive vertices** such as *B*, *D* or *A*, *C*.

A polygon is either convex or concave. It is **convex** if all the interior angles are less than 180° and all the diagonals appear in the interior of the figure. It is **concave** if at least one interior angle is greater than 180° and at least one diagonal falls outside the figure. In the concave polygon (figure B), the diagonal *HJ* is outside the figure.

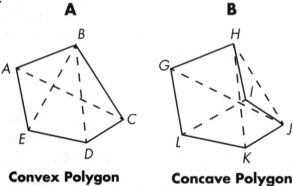

Convex Polygon   **Concave Polygon**

Name all pairs of nonconsecutive vertices in each polygon. Then, draw all the diagonals. Label each polygon as *concave* or *convex*.

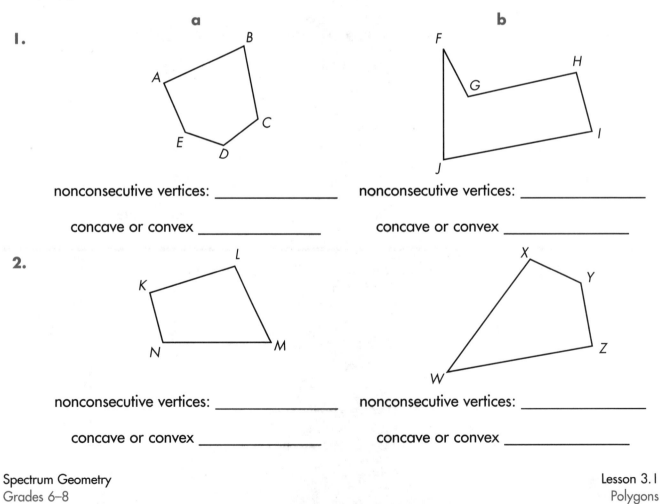

a

1.

nonconsecutive vertices: _____

concave or convex _____

b

nonconsecutive vertices: _____

concave or convex _____

2.

nonconsecutive vertices: _____

concave or convex _____

nonconsecutive vertices: _____

concave or convex _____

Lesson 3.2   Quadrilaterals

A **quadrilateral** is a closed figure with 4 sides. It has 4 vertices. The sum of the angle measures of a quadrilateral is 360°.

A **parallelogram** is a quadrilateral whose opposite sides are parallel and congruent.

A **rectangle** is a parallelogram with four right angles.

A **square** has four right angles and four congruent sides. (A square is a special kind of rectangle and a special kind of rhombus.)

A **rhombus** is a parallelogram with four congruent sides. Opposite sides are parallel and opposite angles are equal.

A **trapezoid** is a quadrilateral with only one pair of parallel sides, called *bases*. Nonparallel sides are called *legs*.

A **kite** has two pairs of congruent adjacent sides but no parallel sides.

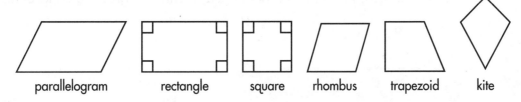

| parallelogram | rectangle | square | rhombus | trapezoid | kite |

Use the figures to answer each question.

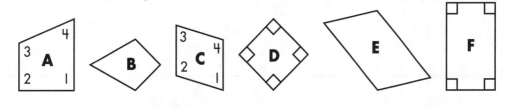

1. Write three names for figure D. _____ _____ _____

2. Write two names for figure F. _____ _____

3. Describe a difference between figures D and F. _____

4. What is the name for figure A? _____

5. In figure A, ∠1 and ∠2 are 90°, and ∠3 is 115°. What is the measure of ∠4? _____ °

6. Write two names for figure C. _____ _____

7. In figure C, if ∠1 is 70°, what is the measure of ∠3? _____ °

8. Name figure B. _____

Lesson 3.3 Similar Figures

Two figures are **similar** if their corresponding angles are congruent and the lengths of their corresponding sides are proportional. Write a ratio to determine if the sides are proportional.

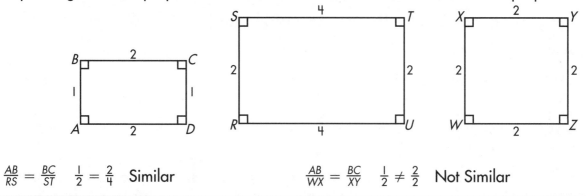

$\frac{AB}{RS} = \frac{BC}{ST}$ $\frac{1}{2} = \frac{2}{4}$ Similar

$\frac{AB}{WX} = \frac{BC}{XY}$ $\frac{1}{2} \neq \frac{2}{2}$ Not Similar

For each pair of figures, write ratios to determine if the sides are proportional. Then, write *similar* or *not similar*. Note: In the figures, the angle marks indicate which angles are congruent.

	a	b

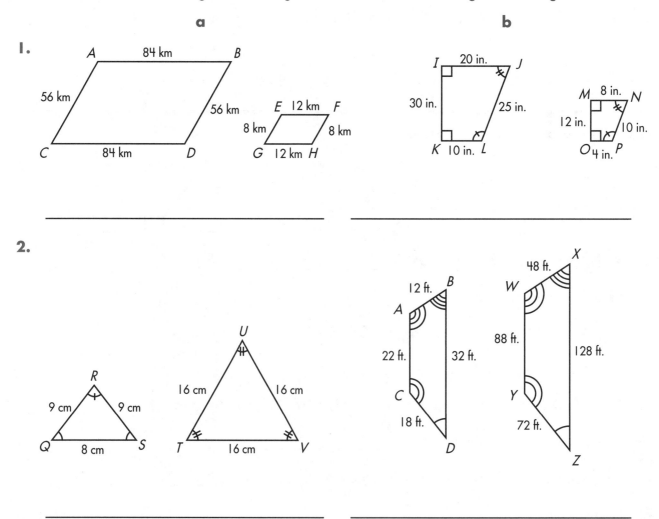

1.

_____   _____

2.

_____   _____

Check What You Learned

Polygons

Write the name for each regular polygon. Find the sum of all of its angles and the measure of one angle.

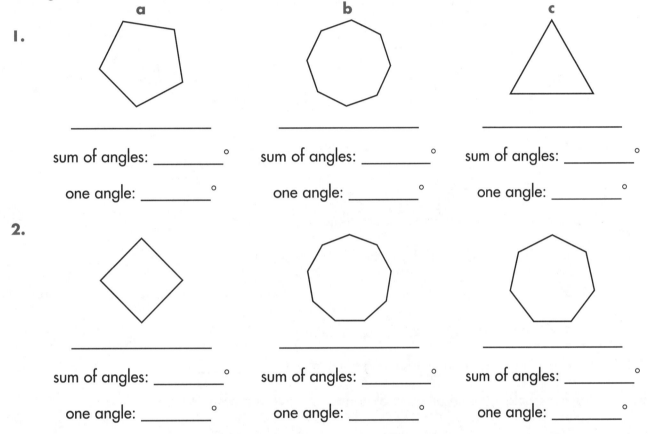

	a	b	c

1.

_____   _____   _____

sum of angles: _____°   sum of angles: _____°   sum of angles: _____°

one angle: _____°   one angle: _____°   one angle: _____°

2.

_____   _____   _____

sum of angles: _____°   sum of angles: _____°   sum of angles: _____°

one angle: _____°   one angle: _____°   one angle: _____°

Write the name for each polygon. Label it as *equiangular*, *equilateral*, or *regular*.

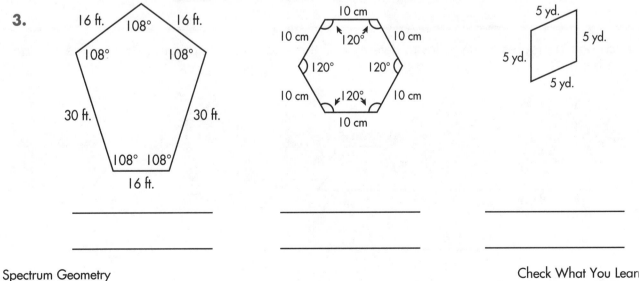

3.   16 ft.   108°   16 ft.

108°   108°

30 ft.   30 ft.

108°   108°

16 ft.

10 cm

10 cm   120°   10 cm

120°   120°

10 cm   120°   10 cm

10 cm

5 yd.

5 yd.

5 yd.

5 yd.

_____   _____   _____

_____   _____   _____

Check What You Learned

Polygons

Use the figures to complete the statements and answer the questions.

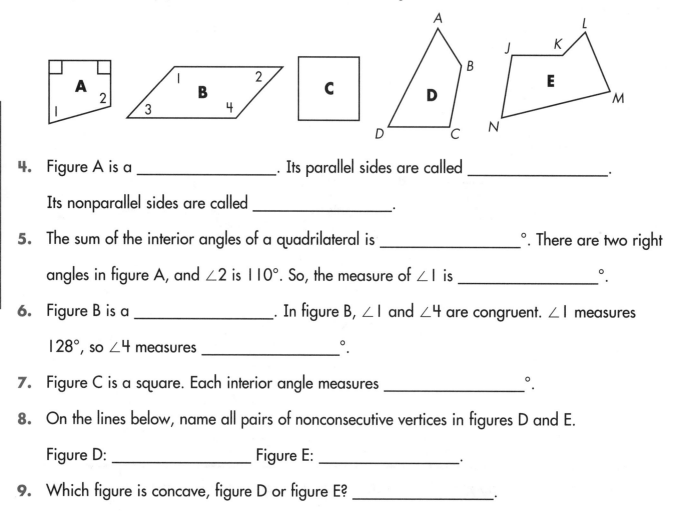

4. Figure A is a _____. Its parallel sides are called _____.

   Its nonparallel sides are called _____.

5. The sum of the interior angles of a quadrilateral is _____°. There are two right

   angles in figure A, and ∠2 is 110°. So, the measure of ∠1 is _____°.

6. Figure B is a _____. In figure B, ∠1 and ∠4 are congruent. ∠1 measures

   128°, so ∠4 measures _____°.

7. Figure C is a square. Each interior angle measures _____°.

8. On the lines below, name all pairs of nonconsecutive vertices in figures D and E.

   Figure D: _____ Figure E: _____.

9. Which figure is concave, figure D or figure E? _____.

For each pair of figures, write ratios to determine if the sides are proportional. Then, write *similar* or *not similar*.

10.

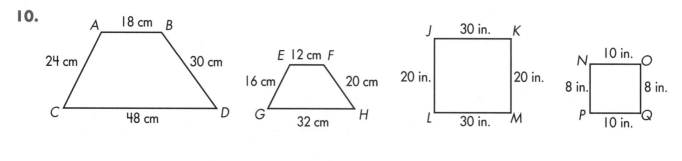

_____ _____

Mid-Test Chapters 1–3

Use the figure to complete the following problems.

1. Is *BF* a line, a line segment, or a ray? _____

2. Name two sets of collinear points. _____, _____

3. Is ∠*GBF* an acute angle, an obtuse angle, or a right angle? _____

4. Name an angle that is vertical to ∠*ABG*. _____

5. Name an angle that is complementary to ∠*EBF*. _____

6. ∠*CBE* is 90°. $\overrightarrow{BD}$ bisects ∠*CBE*. What is the angle measure of ∠*DBE*? _____

7. Name the two angles that are supplementary to ∠*ABC*. _____

Use the figure to complete the following problems.

8. Name the alternate interior angles.

   ∠_____/∠_____   ∠_____/∠_____

9. Name the alternate exterior angles.

   ∠_____/∠_____   ∠_____/∠_____

10. ∠5 and ∠6 are adjacent. If ∠6 is 70°, what is the measure of ∠5? _____

11. Name the transversal of $\overleftrightarrow{HJ}$ and $\overleftrightarrow{KM}$. _____

12. Name an adjacent angle to ∠3. _____

Mid-Test Chapters 1–3

Use the angles and side lengths to create triangles. Label the measures on your drawing.

13. angles: 40° and 80°
side between: 1 inch

14. sides: 1 inch and 2 inches
angle between: 60°

15. sides: 2 inches, 2 inches, 3 inches

16. sides: 4 cm, 5 cm, 6 cm

Write a proportion for each problem. Then, solve the problem.

17. Members of the school band are selling apple pies at $14 per pie. How many pies must they sell in order to make $700?

_____ The band members must sell _____ pies.

18. Maria wants to make a scale drawing of her bedroom. The scale is 2 cm = 1 foot. If her bedroom is 14 feet long by 12 feet wide, what is the length and width of her scale drawing?

_____ The length is _____ cm, and the width is _____ cm.

Mid-Test Chapters 1–3

Calculate the missing angle measures. Indicate whether the triangle is *acute*, *right*, or *obtuse*.

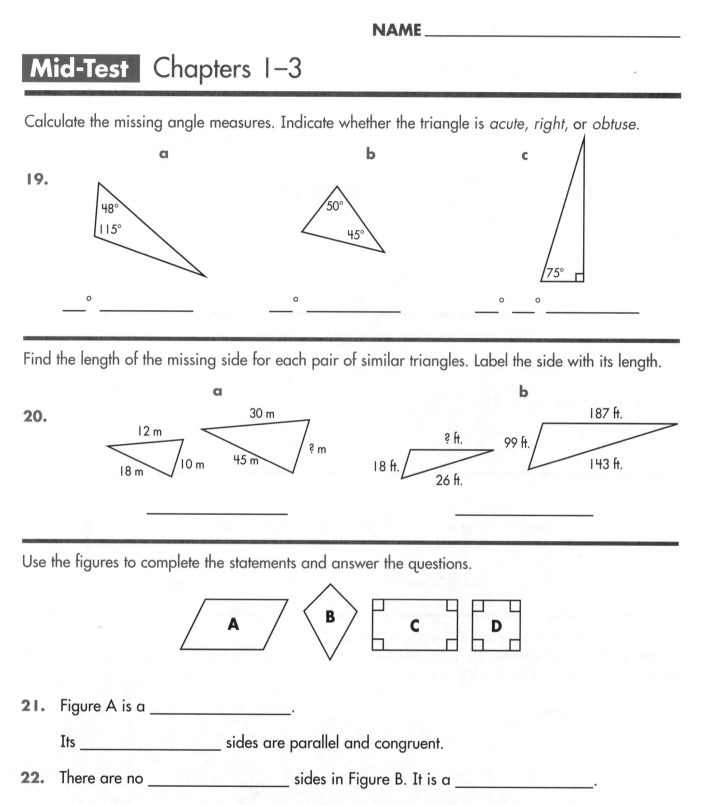

	a	b	c
19.	48° 115°	50° 45°	75°

___° _____   ___° _____   ___° ___° _____

Find the length of the missing side for each pair of similar triangles. Label the side with its length.

a   **b**

20.

12 m   30 m
18 m   10 m   45 m   ? m

? ft.   187 ft.
18 ft.   99 ft.
26 ft.   143 ft.

_____   _____

Use the figures to complete the statements and answer the questions.

A   B   C   D

21. Figure A is a _____.

Its _____ sides are parallel and congruent.

22. There are no _____ sides in Figure B. It is a _____.

23. Figure C is a _____ which is a type of _____.

24. Figure D is a _____.

It differs from figure C in that all four of its sides are _____.

Mid-Test Chapters 1–3

Check whether the triangles are proportional.
Circle *similar* or *not similar*.

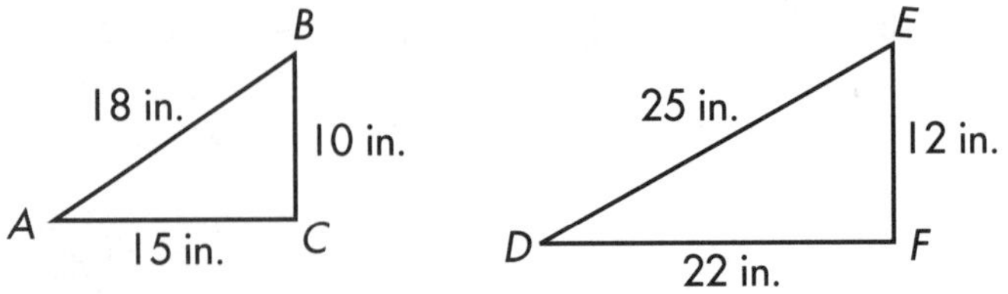

25. $\dfrac{AB}{DE} =$ _____ = _____

 $\dfrac{BC}{EF} =$ _____ = _____

 $\dfrac{AC}{DF} =$ _____ = _____

similar   not similar

Use the Pythagorean Theorem to determine the length of *a*, *b*, or *c*.

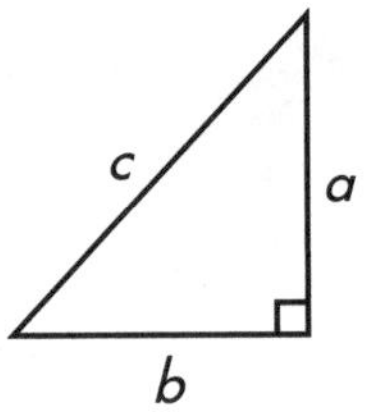

26. If $a = 13$ and $c = 15$, $b = \sqrt{\rule{1.5cm}{0pt}}$ or _____.

27. If $a = 8$ and $b = 6$, $c = \sqrt{\rule{1.5cm}{0pt}}$ or _____.

28. If $b = 121$ and $c = 196$, $a = \sqrt{\rule{1.5cm}{0pt}}$ or _____.

Solve.

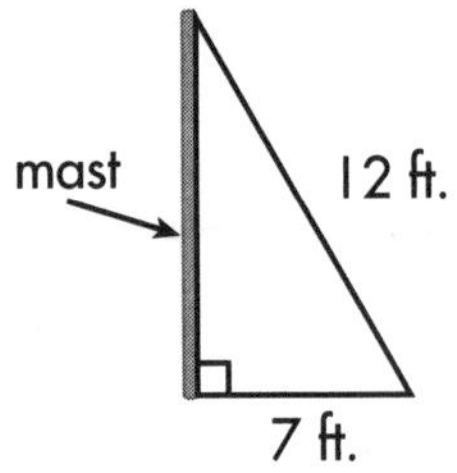

29. Miranda's sailboat needs a new sail. If the sail is 7 feet wide and measures 12 feet long, how tall must the mast be?

 _____ The mast must be _____ feet.

Find the distance between each of the points given below using the Pythagorean Theorem. Round answers to the nearest hundredth.

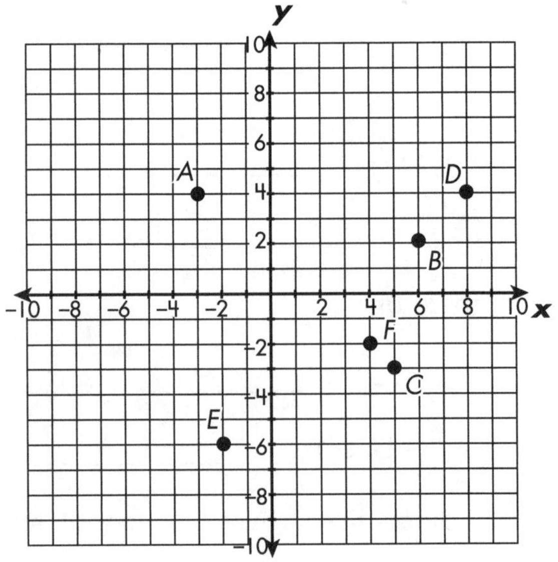

30. $AB =$ _____

31. $CD =$ _____

32. $EF =$ _____

Check What You Know

The Coordinate Plane

Add or subtract the following integers.

	a	**b**	**c**
1.	$2 - 18 =$ _____	$-7 - (-7) =$ _____	$-15 + (-6) =$ _____
2.	$-3 - (-9) =$ _____	$2 + 3 =$ _____	$7 - 18 =$ _____
3.	$10 + 4 =$ _____	$-17 + (-3) =$ _____	$-5 + 14 =$ _____
4.	$12 + (-5) =$ _____	$4 - 9 =$ _____	$-2 + 2 =$ _____

Use the grid to name the point for each ordered pair.

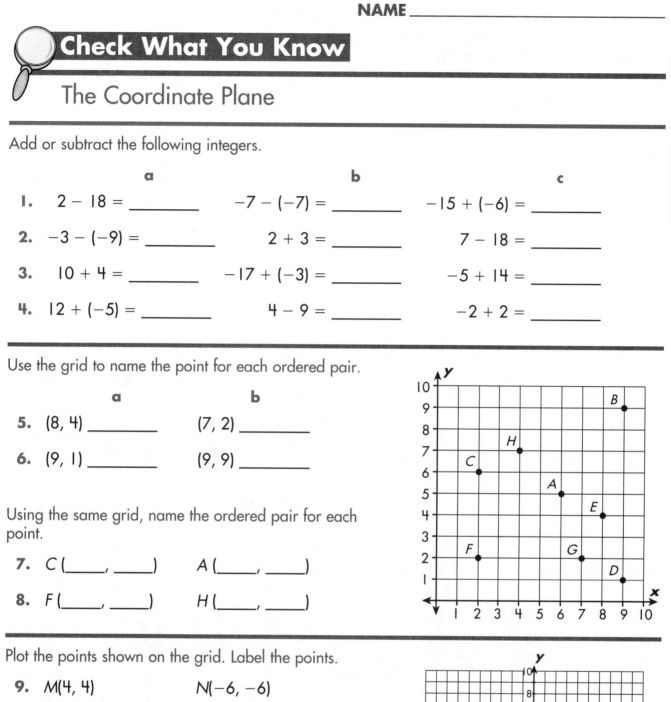

	a	**b**
5.	$(8, 4)$ _____	$(7, 2)$ _____
6.	$(9, 1)$ _____	$(9, 9)$ _____

Using the same grid, name the ordered pair for each point.

7. C (____, ____)   A (____, ____)

8. F (____, ____)   H (____, ____)

Plot the points shown on the grid. Label the points.

9. M(4, 4)   N(−6, −6)

10. O(−4, 6)   P(5, −4)

11. Q(−3, −3)   R(9, 2)

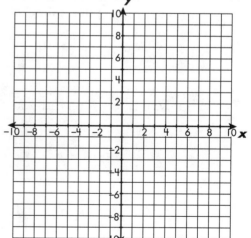

NAME _____

Check What You Know

The Coordinate Plane

12. Is the transformation shown in the grid a translation, rotation, reflection, or dilation?

_____

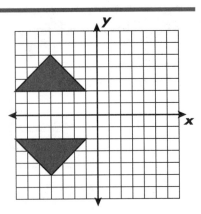

13. What are the coordinates of the preimage?

A(_____, _____), B(_____, _____),

C(_____, _____), D(_____, _____)

14. What are the coordinates of the image?

A'(_____, _____), B'(_____, _____),

C'(_____, _____), D'(_____, _____)

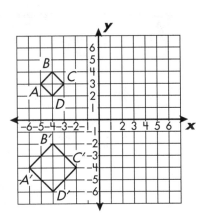

15. Which transformation was performed on this figure?

_____

16. Plot the following coordinates on the grid at right and connect the points with straight lines.

A(−8, 5), B(−6, 7), C(−4, 5), D(−4, 2), E(−8, 2)

17. What type of polygon did you draw?

_____

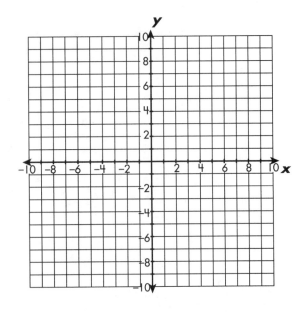

Lesson 4.1 Working with Integers

Integers are the set of whole numbers and their opposites. **Positive integers** are greater than zero. **Negative integers** are less than zero, and they are always less than positive integers.

Negative Integers										Positive Integers

–10 –9 –8 –7 –6 –5 –4 –3 –2 –1 0 1 2 3 4 5 6 7 8 9 10

The sum of two positive integers is a positive integer.

$4 + 3 = 7$

The sum of two negative integers is a negative integer.

$-4 + (-3) = -7$

To find the sum of a positive and negative integer, first find their absolute values. **Absolute value** is the distance (in units) that a number is from 0 expressed as a positive quantity. It is written as $|x|$.

To add -4 and 3, find the absolute values.

$|-4| = 4$

$|3| = 3$

$4 - 3 = -1$

Then, subtract the lesser number from the greater number. The sum has the same sign as the integer with the larger absolute value.

Since 4 is negative, the answer is negative.

$5 - 7 = 5 + (-7) = -2$

Add or subtract.

	a	**b**	**c**
1.	$6 + 3 =$ _____	$10 + (-2) =$ _____	$-5 + 13 =$ _____
2.	$2 - 9 =$ _____	$-3 - 6 =$ _____	$7 - (-5) =$ _____
3.	$-35 - 0 =$ _____	$-2 + (-7) =$ _____	$-13 + (-7) =$ _____
4.	$7 - 19 =$ _____	$11 + (-33) =$ _____	$12 - 23 =$ _____
5.	$-4 + 4 =$ _____	$-1 + 3 =$ _____	$9 + (-8) =$ _____
6.	$-5 + (-5) =$ _____	$10 - (-1) =$ _____	$-13 - 6 =$ _____

Lesson 4.2 Plotting Ordered Pairs

The position of any point on a grid can be described by an **ordered pair** of numbers. The two numbers are named in order: (x, y). Point A on the grid at the right is named by the ordered pair (3, 2). It is located at 3 on the horizontal scale (x) and 2 on the vertical scale (y). The number on the horizontal scale is always named first in an ordered pair. Point B is named by the ordered pair (7, 3).

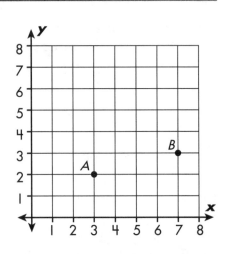

Use Grid I to name the point or ordered pair.

1. (7, 2) _____   (3, 4) _____

2. (3, 6) _____   (9, 6) _____

3. L (____ , ____)   C (____ , ____)

4. J (____ , ____)   I (____ , ____)

5. F (____ , ____)   K (____ , ____)

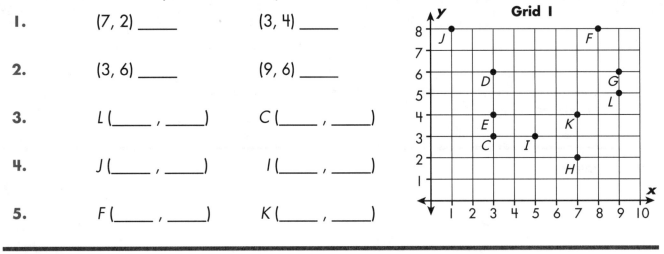

Plot the four points on Grid 2. Label each point.

6. (1, 5) _____   (5, 3) _____

7. (7, 4) _____   (2, 2) _____

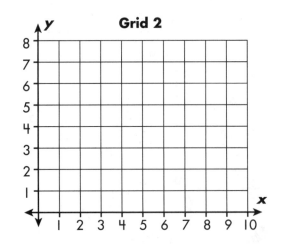

Lesson 4.2 Plotting Ordered Pairs

A **coordinate plane** is formed by two intersecting number lines. The **x-axis** is the horizontal line. The **y-axis** is the vertical line. The **origin** is located at the ordered pair (0, 0). The coordinate plane is divided into four quadrants, which are named in counterclockwise order, as shown on the right.

Ordered pairs are listed as (x, y). These two numbers show the distance from the ordered pair to the origin, along the x- and y-axes.

On the right, Point A is located at (4, 2). Point B is located at (−5, −3).

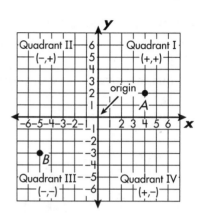

Plot each ordered pair on Grid 1.

Grid 1

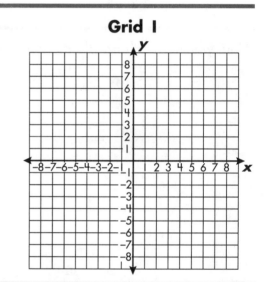

1. A(4, 5)   B(−4, −3)

2. C(2, −3)   D(−3, 2)

3. E(7, 1)   F(−7, 8)

4. G(6, −4)   H(−6, −7)

5. I(1, 1)   J(4, −7)

Write where each lettered point is located on Grid 2.

Grid 2

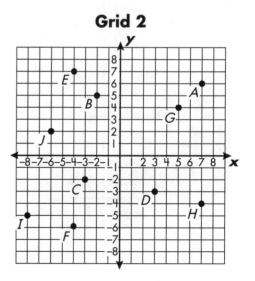

6. A(____, ____)   B(____, ____)

7. C(____, ____)   D(____, ____)

8. E(____, ____)   F(____, ____)

9. G(____, ____)   H(____, ____)

10. I(____, ____)   J(____, ____)

NAME _____

Lesson 4.3   Transformations

A **transformation** is a change in the position or size of a figure. In a **translation**, a figure slides in any direction. In a **rotation**, a figure is turned about a point. In a **reflection**, a figure is flipped over a line. In a **dilation**, a figure is enlarged or reduced. One way to view a figure and its transformation is to graph it on a coordinate plane, as shown below.

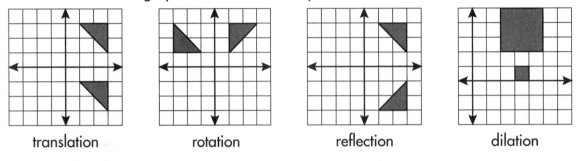

| translation | rotation | reflection | dilation |

Write whether each transformation is a *translation*, *rotation*, *reflection*, or *dilation*.

| a | b | c |

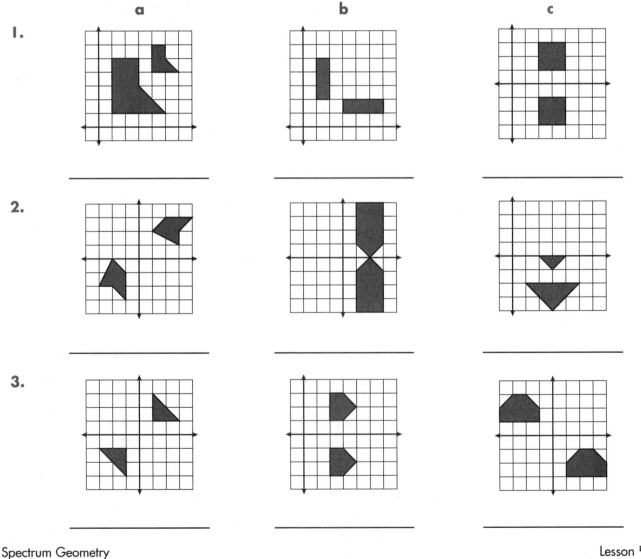

1. _____ _____ _____

2. _____ _____ _____

3. _____ _____ _____

Lesson 4.4 Transformations: Translations

A **transformation** is a change in the position or size of a figure.

A **translation** is a slide of a figure. The figure can be slid up, down, or sideways. However, the size, shape, and orientation of the figure remain the same.

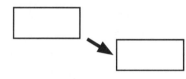 This figure has been translated down and to the right.

State if the figures below represent a translation by writing *yes* or *no*.

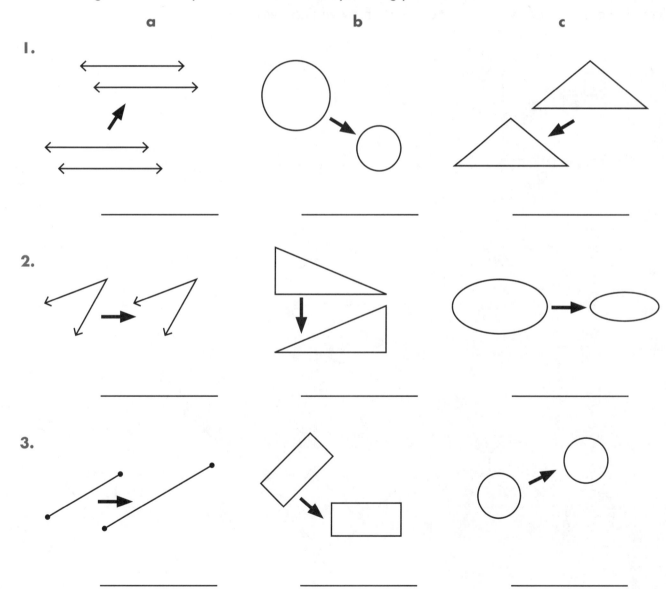

	a	b	c

1.

2.

3.

Lesson 4.5 Transformations: Reflections

A **transformation** is a change in the position or size of a figure.

A **reflection** is a flip of a figure. It can be flipped to the side, up, or down.

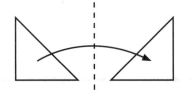 This figure has been flipped horizontally over the dotted line.

State if the figures below represent a reflection by writing *yes* or *no*.

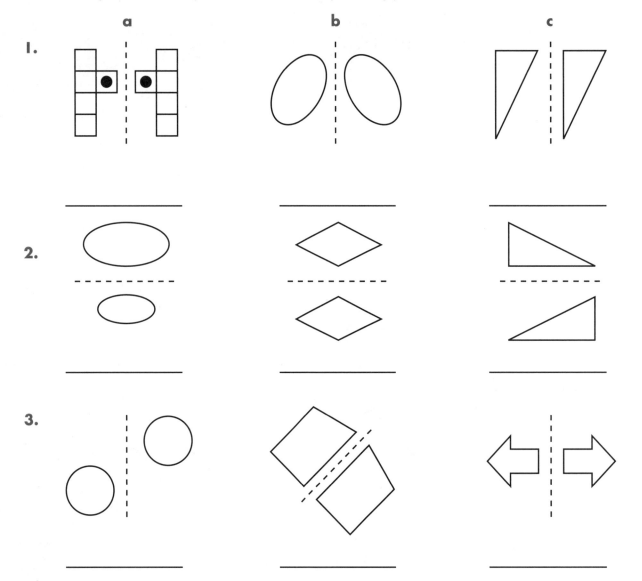

      a   b   c

1.

2.

3.

Lesson 4.6 Transformations: Rotations

A **transformation** is a change in the position or size of a figure.

A **rotation** is a turn of a figure. The figure can be rotated any number of degrees.

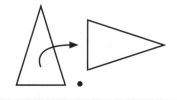 This figure has been rotated 90° clockwise about the point. This point is called the **center of rotation**.

State if the figures below represent a rotation by writing *yes* or *no*.

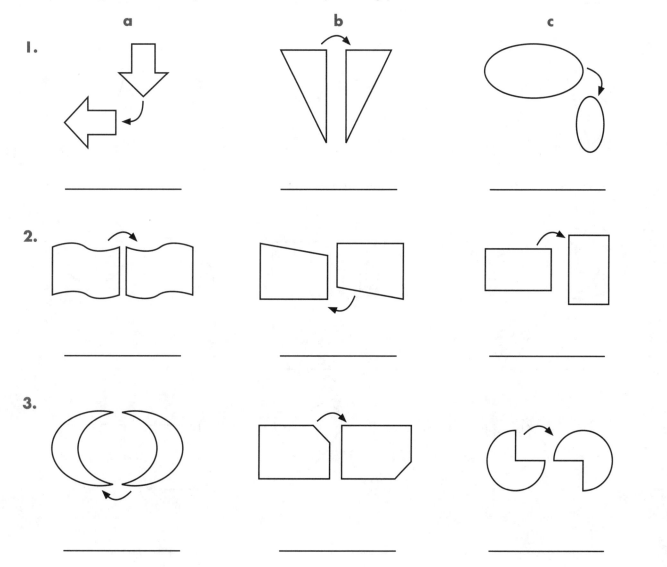

Lesson 4.7 Transformations: Translations, Reflections, and Rotations

State if the figures below represent a *translation*, *reflection*, or *rotation*.

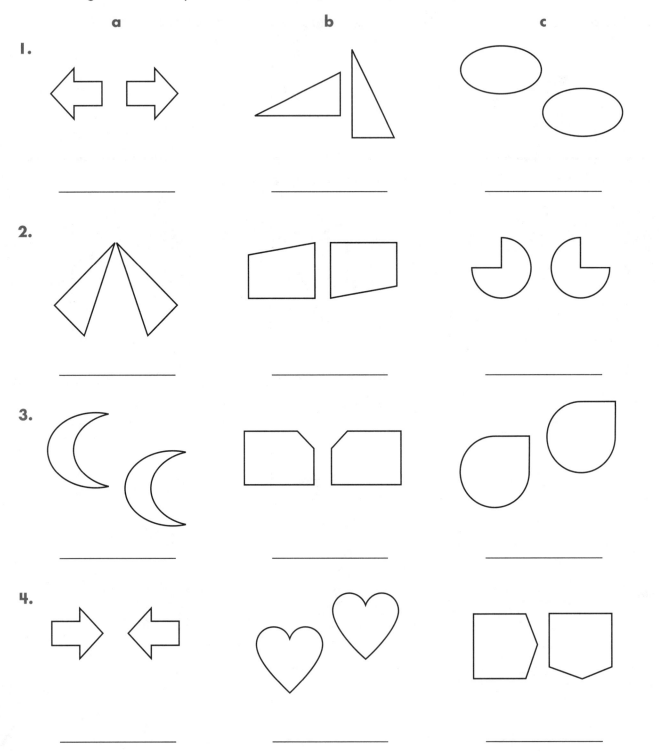

a   b   c

1. _____   _____   _____

2. _____   _____   _____

3. _____   _____   _____

4. _____   _____   _____

Lesson 4.8 Congruence

Two shapes are said to be **congruent** if they are the same size and shape regardless of orientation. If a figure is **rotated**, **translated**, or **reflected** over a line, the two resulting shapes are congruent.

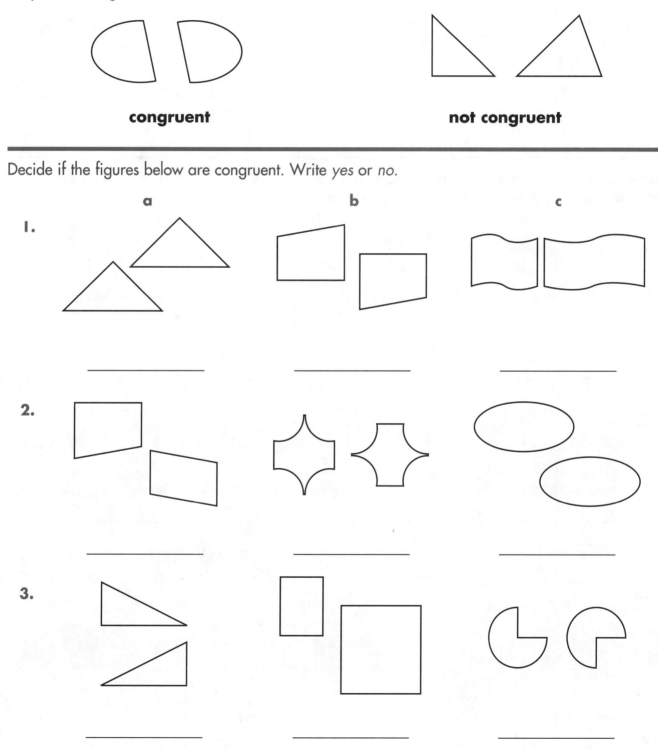

congruent   **not congruent**

Decide if the figures below are congruent. Write *yes* or *no*.

	a	b	c
1.			

2.		

3.		

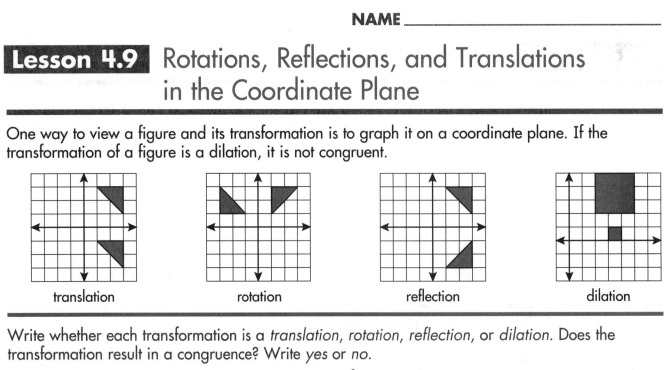

Lesson 4.9 Rotations, Reflections, and Translations in the Coordinate Plane

One way to view a figure and its transformation is to graph it on a coordinate plane. If the transformation of a figure is a dilation, it is not congruent.

translation   rotation   reflection   dilation

Write whether each transformation is a *translation*, *rotation*, *reflection*, or *dilation*. Does the transformation result in a congruence? Write *yes* or *no*.

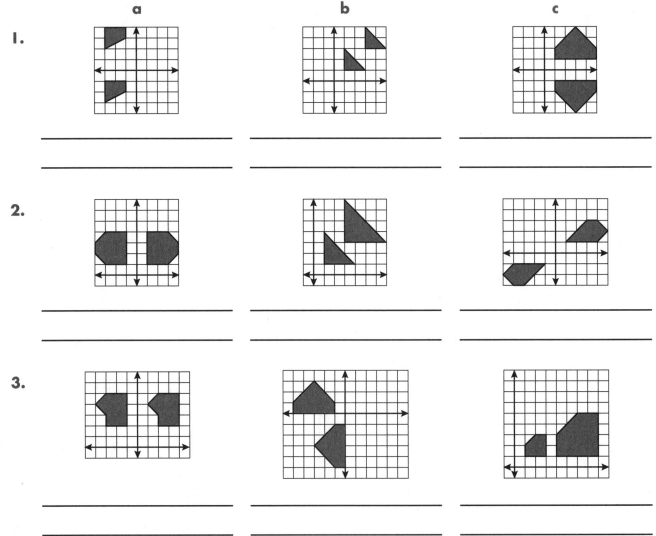

	a	b	c
1.			
2.			
3.			

Lesson 4.9 Rotations, Reflections, and Translations in the Coordinate Plane

Graphing figures on a coordinate plane helps show how they are transformed. The original figure is called a **preimage**. The transformed figure is called the **image**. Read the numbers on the x-axis and y-axis to determine the location of the figure.

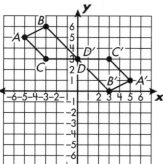

This figure has been rotated 180° about one point of the figure. As a result, the preimage and the image share a point. The 4 corners of the preimage are points A, B, C, and D. The four corners of the image are also labeled A′, B′, C′, and D′, but note the prime symbol (′) after each.

The coordinates of the preimage are: A (−5, 5), B (−3, 6) C (−3, 3), D (0, 3).

The coordinates of the image are: A′(5, 1), B′(3, 0), C′(3, 3), D′(0, 3).

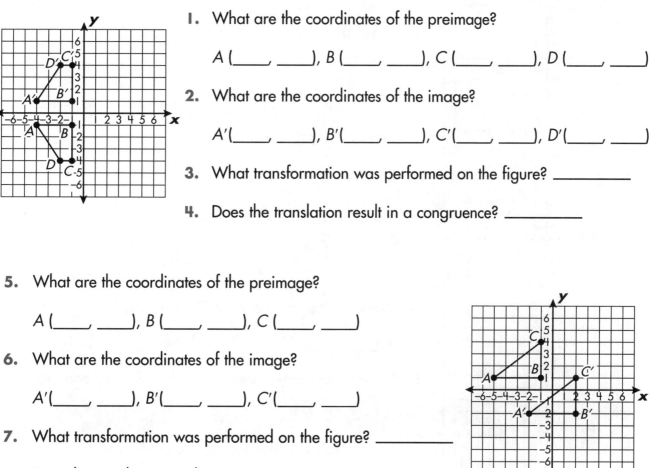

1. What are the coordinates of the preimage?

   A (____, ____), B (____, ____), C (____, ____), D (____, ____)

2. What are the coordinates of the image?

   A′(____, ____), B′(____, ____), C′(____, ____), D′(____, ____)

3. What transformation was performed on the figure? _____

4. Does the translation result in a congruence? _____

5. What are the coordinates of the preimage?

   A (____, ____), B (____, ____), C (____, ____)

6. What are the coordinates of the image?

   A′(____, ____), B′(____, ____), C′(____, ____)

7. What transformation was performed on the figure? _____

8. Does the translation result in a congruence? _____

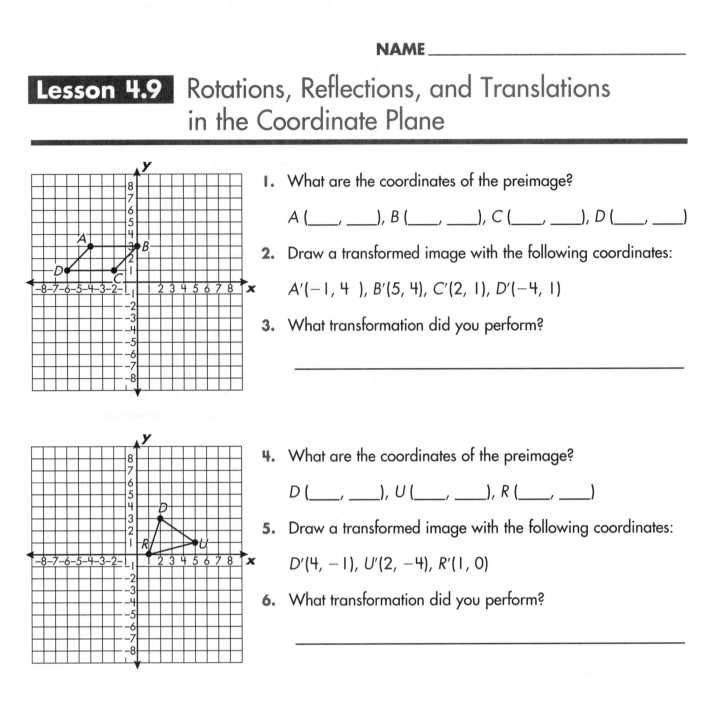

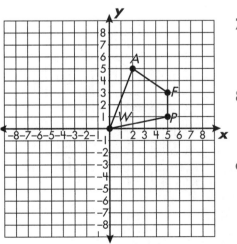

Lesson 4.9 Rotations, Reflections, and Translations in the Coordinate Plane

NAME _____

1. What are the coordinates of the preimage?

   A (____, ____), B (____, ____), C (____, ____), D (____, ____)

2. Draw a transformed image with the following coordinates:

   A′(−1, 4), B′(5, 4), C′(2, 1), D′(−4, 1)

3. What transformation did you perform?

   _____

4. What are the coordinates of the preimage?

   D (____, ____), U (____, ____), R (____, ____)

5. Draw a transformed image with the following coordinates:

   D′(4, −1), U′(2, −4), R′(1, 0)

6. What transformation did you perform?

   _____

7. What are the coordinates of the preimage?

   A (____, ____), W ((____, ____), F (____, ____), P (____, ____)

8. Draw a transformed image with the following coordinates:

   A′(−2, 5), W′(0, 0), F′(−5, 3), P′(−5, 1)

9. What transformation did you perform?

   _____

Lesson 4.10 Transformation Sequences

If there exists a sequence of translations, reflections, rotations, and/or dilations that will transform one figure into the other, the two figures are either **similar** or **congruent**. Similar figures are the same shape but not the same size while congruent shapes are both the same shape and the same size. Follow the sequence of transformations to determine if two figures are similar or congruent.

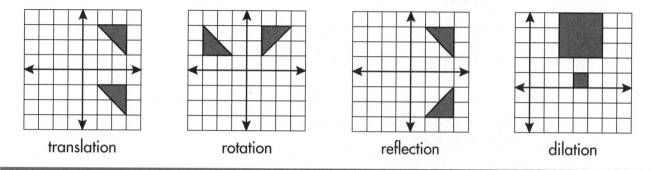

translation   rotation   reflection   dilation

Determine if a set of transformations exist between figures 1 and 2. Then, write *similar*, *congruent*, or *neither*.

a   b   c

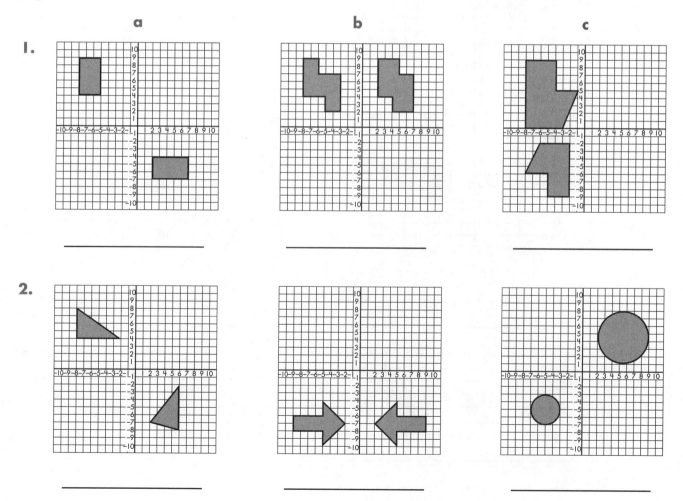

1. _____   _____   _____

2. _____   _____   _____

Lesson 4.10 Transformation Sequences

Sometimes, the order of the steps in a transformation sequence will vary, but every shape has a specific sequence it must go through in order to be transformed.

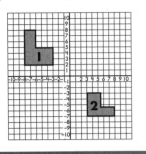

Step 1: The figure is reflected across the y-axis.

Step 2: The figure is rotated 90° counterclockwise.

Step 3: The figure is translated by −8 along the y-axis.

Step 4: The figure is decreased by 20%.

Write the steps each figure must go through to be transformed from figure 1 to figure 2. Are the figures *similar*, *congruent*, or *neither*?

a

b

1.

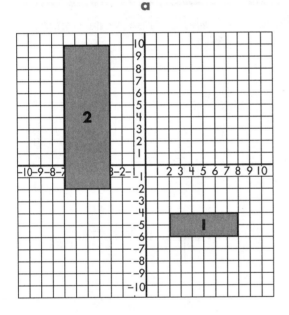

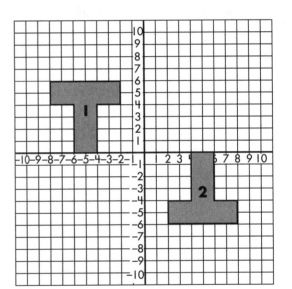

_____

_____

_____

_____

_____

_____

_____

_____

_____

_____

_____

_____

Lesson 4.11 Drawing Shapes

A **polygon** is a closed shape created by straight lines. The **vertices** of a polygon are the points where the lines intersect. These vertices can be described by coordinates and plotted on a coordinate plane. When the points are connected by straight lines, they form a polygon.

The points $A(-6, 3)$, $B(-3, 6)$, and $C(-3, 1)$ are plotted on a coordinate plane. When the points are connected with straight lines, they form a triangle, a type of polygon.

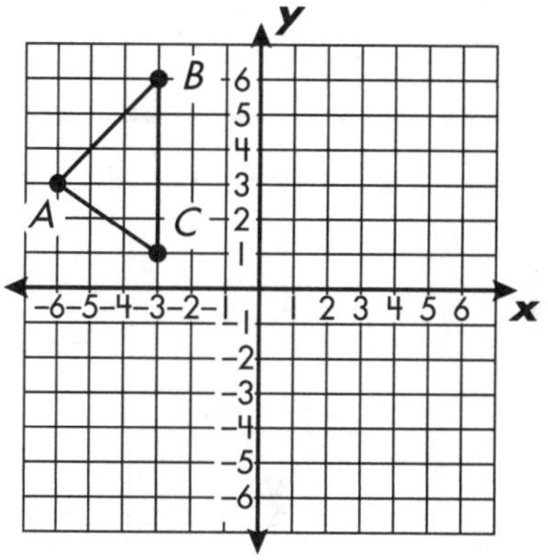

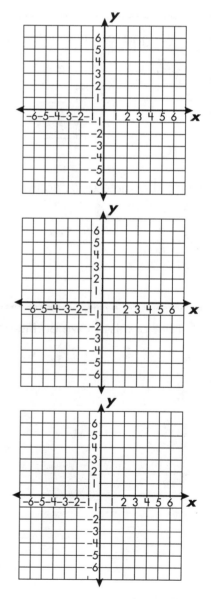

Plot the points on the coordinate plane and connect the points with straight lines.

1. $A(-2, 3)$, $B(2, 3)$, $C(-4, -2)$, $D(4, -2)$

   Which type of polygon did you draw?

   _____

2. $E(1, -3)$, $F(5, -1)$, $G(5, -5)$, $H(4, -3)$

   Which type of polygon did you draw?

   _____

3. $I(-3, 5)$, $J(4, 5)$, $K(1, 2)$, $L(-6, 2)$

   Which type of polygon did you draw?

   _____

Check What You Learned

The Coordinate Plane

Add or subtract the following integers.

| | **a** | **b** | **c** |

1. $5 + 9 =$ _____ $12 - 15 =$ _____ $-6 + (-20) =$ _____

2. $17 - 23 =$ _____ $-8 - (-4) =$ _____ $7 - 18 =$ _____

3. $13 + 2 =$ _____ $11 - (-6) =$ _____ $-3 + (-6) =$ _____

4. $-5 + 1 =$ _____ $32 - (-9) =$ _____ $6 - 4 =$ _____

Use the grid to name a point for each ordered pair.

a   **b**

5. $(8, 7)$ _____ $(4, 3)$ _____

6. $(1, 7)$ _____ $(3, 5)$ _____

Using the same grid, name the ordered pair for each point.

7. $A(\_\_\_, \_\_\_)$ $H(\_\_\_, \_\_\_)$

8. $F(\_\_\_, \_\_\_)$ $D(\_\_\_, \_\_\_)$

Plot the points shown on the grid. Label the points.

9. $M(-3, -4)$ $N(9, -6)$

10. $O(-5, 7)$ $P(7, -2)$

11. $Q(-7, 2)$ $R(8, 7)$

Spectrum Geometry
Grades 6–8
60

Check What You Learned
Chapter 4

Check What You Learned

The Coordinate Plane

12. Is the transformation shown in the grid a translation, rotation, reflection, or dilation? _____

13. Which transformation was performed on this figure?

_____

14. What are the coordinates of the preimage?

A(_____, _____), B(_____, _____),

C(_____, _____), D(_____, _____)

15. What are the coordinates of the image?

A'(_____, _____), B'(_____, _____),

C'(_____, _____), D'(_____, _____)

16. Plot the following coordinates on the grid and connect the points by straight lines.

A(3, 8), B(6, 8), C(8, 6), D(8, 3),

E(6, 1), F(3, 1), G(1, 3), H(1, 6)

17. What type of polygon did you draw?

_____

NAME _____

Check What You Know

Circles and Solid Figures

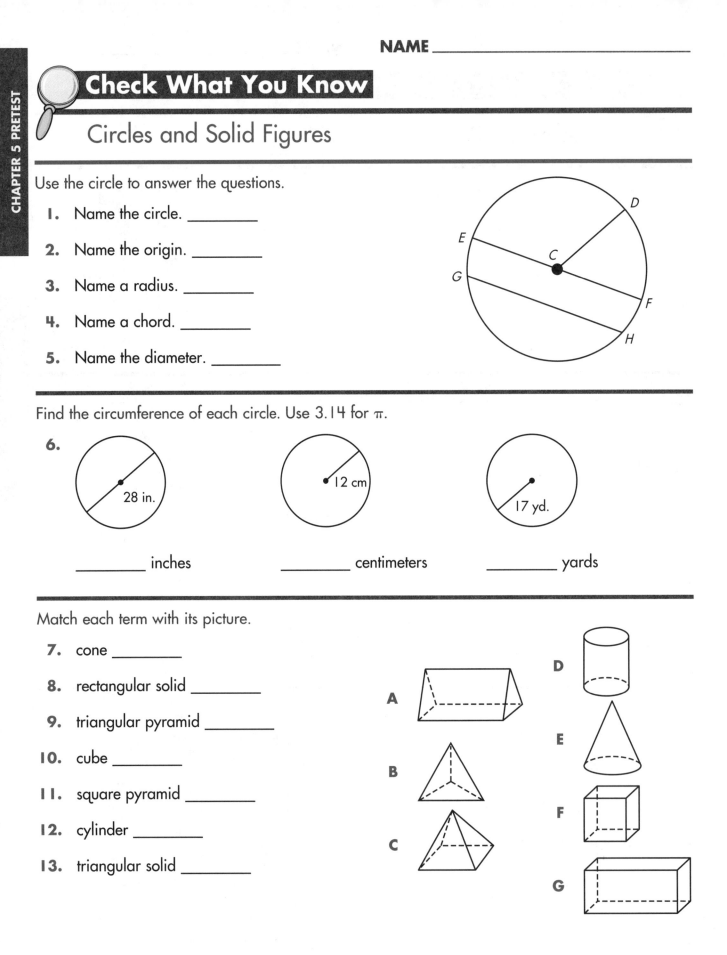

Use the circle to answer the questions.

1. Name the circle. _____

2. Name the origin. _____

3. Name a radius. _____

4. Name a chord. _____

5. Name the diameter. _____

Find the circumference of each circle. Use 3.14 for π.

6.

_____ inches

_____ centimeters

_____ yards

Match each term with its picture.

7. cone _____

8. rectangular solid _____

9. triangular pyramid _____

10. cube _____

11. square pyramid _____

12. cylinder _____

13. triangular solid _____

Check What You Know

Circles and Solid Figures

Answer each question. Use 3.14 for π.

14. Is a line segment with one endpoint at the origin and the other endpoint on the circle called a *chord* or a *radius*?

    It is called a _____.

15. How is a circle named?

    It is named by its _____.

16. If the circumference of a circle is 15.7 feet, what is the diameter? What is the radius?

    The diameter is _____ feet. The radius is _____ feet.

17. On a basketball court, the diameter of the center circle is 12 feet. What is the circle's circumference?

    The circle's circumference is _____ feet.

18. Alex holds a solid figure that has 2 circular bases. Is the figure a cone or a cylinder?

    The solid figure is a _____.

19. A cube has 6 faces. Are the faces rectangular or square?

    The cube's faces are _____.

Lesson 5.1 Circles

A **circle** is a set of points that are all the same distance from a given point, called the center or the **origin**. A circle is named by its origin.

A **radius** of a circle is a line segment with one endpoint at the origin and the other endpoint on the circle.

A **chord** is a line segment with both endpoints on the circle.

A **diameter** is a chord that passes through the origin of the circle.

Name a radius, chord, and diameter of circle *X*.

   radius: $\overline{XZ}$, $\overline{XV}$, or $\overline{XW}$ chord: $\overline{VW}$ or $\overline{SR}$ diameter: $\overline{VW}$

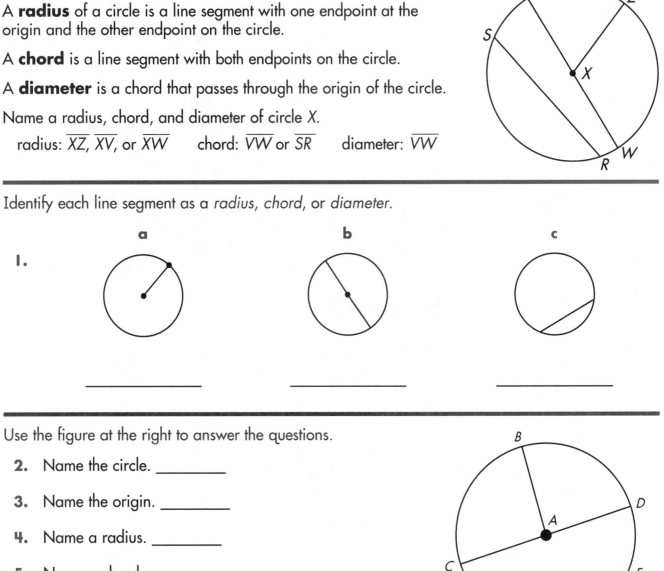

Identify each line segment as a *radius, chord,* or *diameter*.

        a   **b**   **c**

1.

    _____   _____   _____

Use the figure at the right to answer the questions.

  2. Name the circle. _____

  3. Name the origin. _____

  4. Name a radius. _____

  5. Name a chord. _____

  6. Name the diameter. _____

  7. Draw a circle *L*, with radius $\overline{LM}$, diameter $\overline{NO}$, and chord $\overline{RS}$.

Lesson 5.2 Circumference of a Circle

The perimeter of a circle is called the **circumference**.

The relationship between the circumference (C) and the diameter (d) is $C \div d = \pi$. Pi (π) is approximately $3\frac{1}{7}$ or 3.14.

To find the circumference, diameter, or radius of a circle, use the formulas $C = \pi d$ or $C = 2\pi r$.

If the diameter of a circle is 4 cm, the circumference is 4π cm, or about 12.56 cm.

If the radius of a circle is 5 cm, the circumference is $2\pi 5$ cm, or about 31.4 cm.

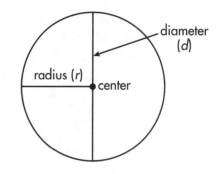

Complete the information for each circle described below. Use 3.14 for π. When necessary, round to the nearest hundredth.

	a Diameter	b Radius	c Circumference
1.	_____ ft.	_____ ft.	9.42 ft.
2.	37 cm	_____ cm	_____ cm
3.	_____ yd.	12 yd.	_____ yd.
4.	4.5 mm	_____ mm	_____ mm
5.	_____ km	_____ km	31.4 km
6.	24.2 in.	_____ in.	_____ in.
7.	_____ mi.	5.25 mi.	_____ mi.
8.	_____ cm	_____ cm	4.71 cm
9.	_____ ft.	4.8 ft.	_____ ft.

Lesson 5.3 Solid Figures

A **solid figure** is a three-dimensional figure. A **face** is a flat surface of a solid figure. An **edge** is the intersection of two faces. A **vertex** is a point where three or more faces meet. A **base** is a face on which the solid figure rests.

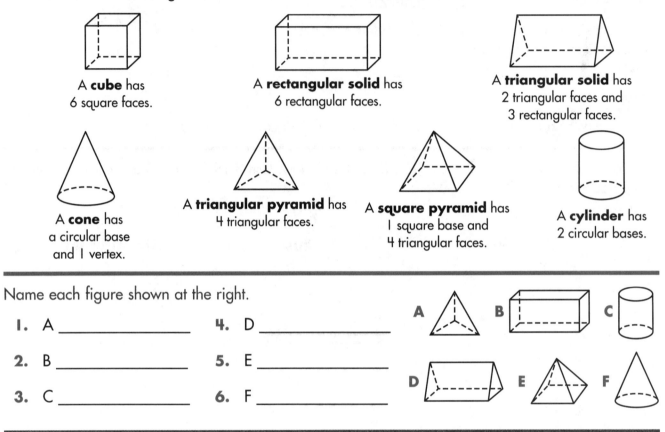

A **cube** has
6 square faces.

A **rectangular solid** has
6 rectangular faces.

A **triangular solid** has
2 triangular faces and
3 rectangular faces.

A **cone** has
a circular base
and 1 vertex.

A **triangular pyramid** has
4 triangular faces.

A **square pyramid** has
1 square base and
4 triangular faces.

A **cylinder** has
2 circular bases.

Name each figure shown at the right.

1. A _____   4. D _____

2. B _____   5. E _____

3. C _____   6. F _____

For the figures above, indicate the number of faces and whether they are *square*, *rectangular*, *triangular*, or *circular*.

	Number of Faces	**Type(s) of Face(s)**
7.	A _____	_____
8.	B _____	_____
9.	C _____	_____
10.	D _____	_____
11.	E _____	_____
12.	F _____	_____

Lesson 5.4 Problem Solving

Answer each question. Use 3.14 for π. If necessary, round answers to the nearest hundredth.

1. Maurice says that a line segment with both endpoints on a circle is called a *radius*. Shaylin says that it is called a *chord*. Who is correct?

   _____ is correct.

2. What is the name of a chord that passes through the origin of a circle?

   The name of this chord is a _____.

3. If the circumference of a circle is 18.84 inches, what is the diameter? What is the radius?

   The diameter is _____ inches. The radius is _____ inches.

4. June draws a chalk circle on the playground that is 2 feet in diameter. What is the circle's circumference?

   The circle's circumference is _____ feet.

5. Padma is holding a solid figure that has 6 square faces. Which kind of solid figure is this?

   The solid figure is a _____.

6. What is the name of a solid figure with 2 circular bases?

   The name of this solid figure is a _____.

Check What You Learned

Circles and Solid Figures

Use the circle to answer the questions.

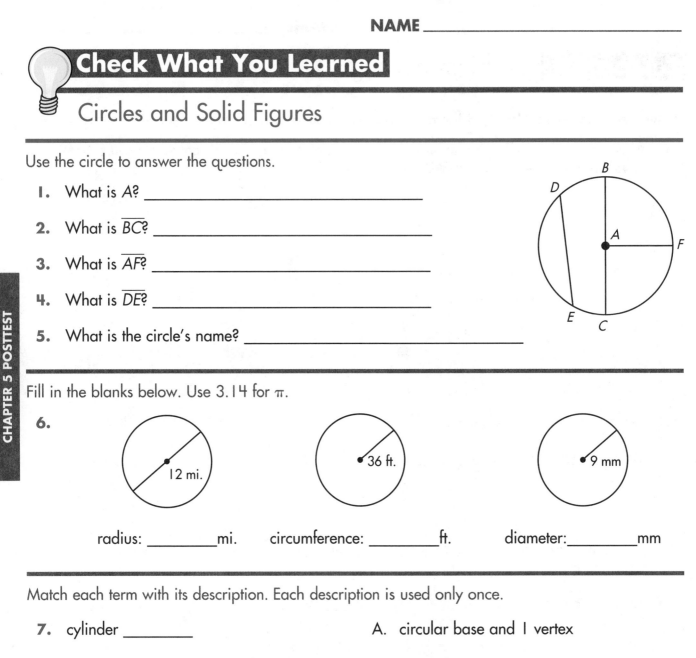

1. What is A? _____

2. What is $\overline{BC}$? _____

3. What is $\overline{AF}$? _____

4. What is $\overline{DE}$? _____

5. What is the circle's name? _____

Fill in the blanks below. Use 3.14 for π.

6.

      12 mi.   36 ft.   9 mm

radius: _____mi.   circumference: _____ft.   diameter:_____mm

Match each term with its description. Each description is used only once.

7. cylinder _____

8. triangular pyramid _____

9. square pyramid _____

10. cone _____

11. rectangular solid _____

12. triangular solid _____

13. cube _____

A. circular base and 1 vertex

B. 6 square faces

C. 2 triangular faces and 3 rectangular faces

D. 2 circular bases

E. 4 triangular faces

F. 6 rectangular faces

G. 1 square base and 4 triangular faces

Check What You Learned

Circles and Solid Figures

Answer each question. Use 3.14 for π.

14. In a circle, which is longer—the radius or the diameter?

The _____ is longer.

15. What is one of the formulas for finding the circumference of a circle?

One of the formulas is _____.

16. If the circumference of a circle is 42.39 cm, what is the diameter? What is the radius?

The diameter is _____ cm. The radius is _____ cm.

17. If the radius of a circle is 3 yards, what is the circle's circumference?

The circle's circumference is _____ yards.

18. What is the difference between a triangular pyramid and a square pyramid?

The difference is _____

_____ .

19. In a solid figure, what is an edge?

An edge is _____ .

NAME _____

Check What You Know

Perimeter and Area

Find the perimeter of each figure.

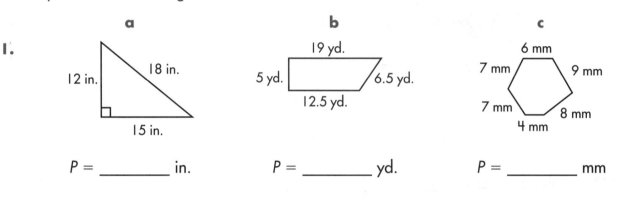

a	b	c

1.

12 in.   18 in.   15 in.

$P =$ _____ in.

19 yd.   5 yd.   6.5 yd.   12.5 yd.

$P =$ _____ yd.

6 mm   7 mm   9 mm   7 mm   8 mm   4 mm

$P =$ _____ mm

Find the unknown measure, area, or perimeter.

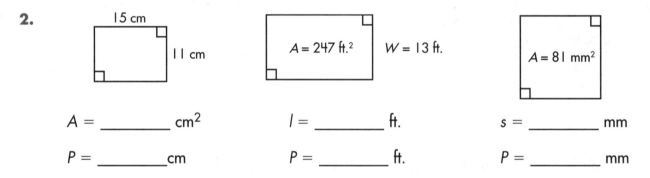

2.

15 cm   11 cm

$A =$ _____ cm^2

$P =$ _____ cm

$A = 247$ ft.^{2} $W = 13$ ft.

$l =$ _____ ft.

$P =$ _____ ft.

$A = 81$ mm^2

$s =$ _____ mm

$P =$ _____ mm

Find the area for the parallelogram or irregular shape.

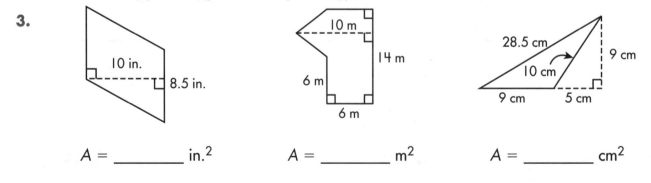

3.

10 in.   8.5 in.

$A =$ _____ in.^{2}

10 m   14 m   6 m   6 m

$A =$ _____ m^2

28.5 cm   9 cm   10 cm   9 cm   5 cm

$A =$ _____ cm^2

Check What You Know

Perimeter and Area

Complete the information for each circle described below. Use 3.14 for π. When necessary, round to the nearest hundredth.

	a Radius	b Diameter	c Area
4.	6 cm	_____ cm	_____ cm^2
5.	_____ ft.	15 ft.	_____ ft.^{2}
6.	_____ in.	_____ in.	78.5 in.^{2}

Find the surface area of each solid figure.

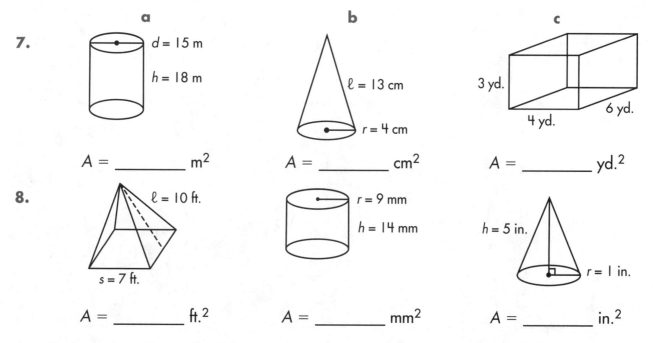

7. **a** $d = 15$ m $h = 18$ m $A = $ _____ m^2

   b $\ell = 13$ cm $r = 4$ cm $A = $ _____ cm^2

   c 3 yd. 6 yd. 4 yd. $A = $ _____ yd.^{2}

8. $\ell = 10$ ft. $s = 7$ ft. $A = $ _____ ft.^{2}

   $r = 9$ mm $h = 14$ mm $A = $ _____ mm^2

   $h = 5$ in. $r = 1$ in. $A = $ _____ in.^{2}

9. Elena needs to wrap a birthday present that is 23 cm long, 11.5 cm wide, and 6 cm high. What is the area of wrapping paper that she will need?

   Elena will need _____ square centimeters of paper.

10. Keisha is making a round hook rug that is 3 yards in diameter. What is the area of the rug?

   The rug is _____ square yards.

Lesson 6.1 Perimeter

The **perimeter (P)** is the distance around a figure. To find the perimeter, find the sum of the lengths of its sides. If two or more sides are equal, the formula can be simplified with multiplication.

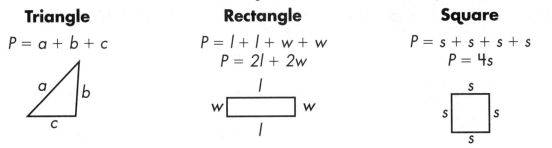

Triangle	Rectangle	Square
$P = a + b + c$	$P = l + l + w + w$ $P = 2l + 2w$	$P = s + s + s + s$ $P = 4s$

In the rectangle above, if the length is 6 cm and the width is 2 cm, the perimeter is:

$P = 2(6 \text{ cm}) + 2(2 \text{ cm}) = 12 \text{ cm} + 4 \text{ cm} = 16 \text{ cm}.$

Find the perimeter of each figure.

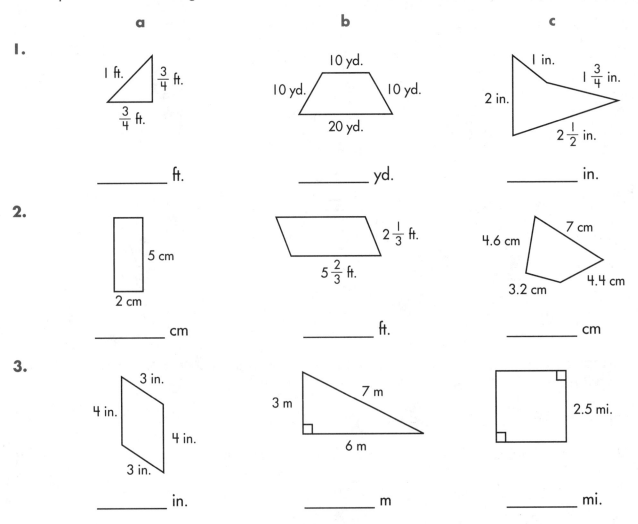

	a	b	c
1.	_____ ft.	_____ yd.	_____ in.
2.	_____ cm	_____ ft.	_____ cm
3.	_____ in.	_____ m	_____ mi.

Lesson 6.2 Area of Rectangles

The **area (A)** of a figure is the number of square units inside that figure. Area is expressed in **square units** or **units²**.

The area of a square or rectangle is the product of its length and width.

$A = l \times w$

$A = 5 \text{ cm} \times 10 \text{ cm}$

$A = 50 \text{ cm}^2$

5 cm ▭ 10 cm

$A = s \times s$

$A = 5 \text{ cm} \times 5 \text{ cm}$

$A = 25 \text{ cm}^2$

5 cm ▢ 5 cm

If you know the area of a rectangle and either the length or width of a side, you can determine the unknown measurement.

$A = l \times w$

$24 \text{ m}^2 = 6 \text{ m} \times w$

$w = 24 \text{ m}^2 / 6 \text{ m}$

$w = 4 \text{ m}$

$A = 24 \text{ m}^2$ 6 cm

Find the area of each rectangle below.

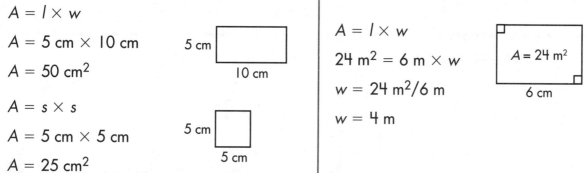

a

1. 2 m / 4 m

_____ m²

b

6 mi. / 6 mi.

_____ mi.²

c

8 ft. / 16 ft.

_____ ft.²

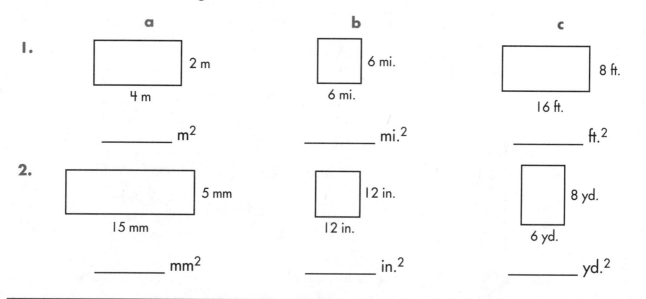

2. 5 mm / 15 mm

_____ mm²

12 in. / 12 in.

_____ in.²

8 yd. / 6 yd.

_____ yd.²

Find the unknown measure for each rectangle below.

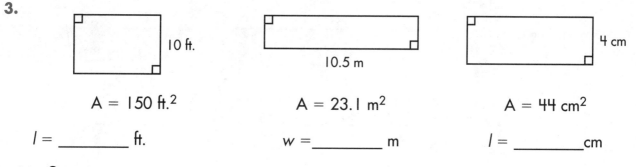

3. 10 ft.

$A = 150 \text{ ft.}^2$

$l =$ _____ ft.

10.5 m

$A = 23.1 \text{ m}^2$

$w =$ _____ m

4 cm

$A = 44 \text{ cm}^2$

$l =$ _____ cm

Lesson 6.3 Area of Parallelograms

A parallelogram is a polygon with two sets of parallel sides. To find the area of a parallelogram, multiply the measure of its base by the measure of its height: $A = b \times h$ or $A = bh$.

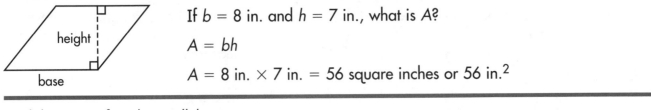

If $b = 8$ in. and $h = 7$ in., what is A?

$A = bh$

$A = 8$ in. $\times 7$ in. $= 56$ square inches or 56 in.^{2}

Find the area of each parallelogram.

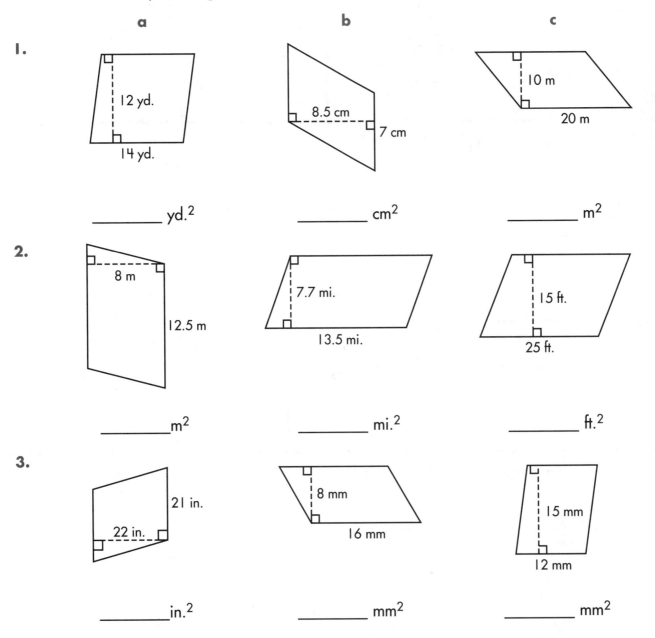

	a	b	c
1.	12 yd. / 14 yd.	8.5 cm / 7 cm	10 m / 20 m
	_____ yd.^{2}	_____ cm^2	_____ m^2
2.	8 m / 12.5 m	7.7 mi. / 13.5 mi.	15 ft. / 25 ft.
	_____ m^2	_____ mi.^{2}	_____ ft.^{2}
3.	21 in. / 22 in.	8 mm / 16 mm	15 mm / 12 mm
	_____ in.^{2}	_____ mm^2	_____ mm^2

Lesson 6.4 Area of Irregular Shapes

To find the area of irregular shapes, separate the shapes into figures for which you can find the area.

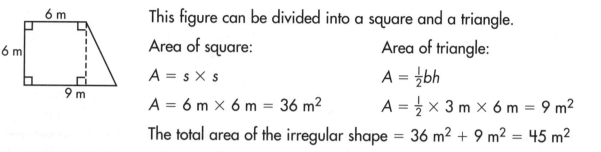

This figure can be divided into a square and a triangle.

Area of square:

$A = s \times s$

$A = 6 \text{ m} \times 6 \text{ m} = 36 \text{ m}^2$

Area of triangle:

$A = \frac{1}{2}bh$

$A = \frac{1}{2} \times 3 \text{ m} \times 6 \text{ m} = 9 \text{ m}^2$

The total area of the irregular shape = $36 \text{ m}^2 + 9 \text{ m}^2 = 45 \text{ m}^2$

Find the area of each figure.

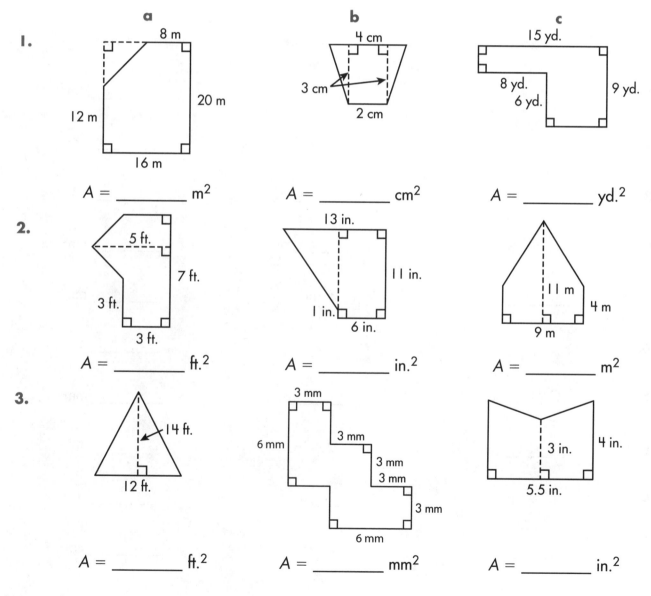

	a	b	c
1.	$A =$ _____ m^2	$A =$ _____ cm^2	$A =$ _____ $yd.^2$
2.	$A =$ _____ $ft.^2$	$A =$ _____ $in.^2$	$A =$ _____ m^2
3.	$A =$ _____ $ft.^2$	$A =$ _____ mm^2	$A =$ _____ $in.^2$

Lesson 6.5 Area of a Circle

The area of a circle is the number of square units it contains. Like circumference, area is calculated using π, which represents about $3\frac{1}{7}$ or 3.14. The formula for finding the area of a circle is:

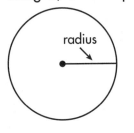

Area = $\pi \times$ radius $\times$ radius

$A = \pi r^2$

If a circle has a radius of 3 in., its area is $\pi \times 3$ in. $\times 3$ in. or about 28.6 in.^{2} If a circle has a diameter of 7 in., its radius is $\frac{1}{2}$ of 7 in., or 3.5 in. In this example, the area = $\pi \times 3.5$ in. $\times 3.5$ in., or about 38.46 in.^{2}

Complete the information for each circle described below. Use 3.14 for π. When necessary, round to the nearest hundredth.

	a Radius	b Diameter	c Area
1.	_____ mm	16 mm	_____ mm^2
2.	_____ ft.	12 ft.	_____ ft.^{2}
3.	4 yd.	_____ yd.	_____ yd.^{2}
4.	9 cm	_____ cm	_____ cm^2
5.	_____ mi.	5 mi.	_____ mi.^{2}
6.	_____ m	26 m	_____ m^2
7.	3.5 mm	_____ mm	_____ mm^2
8.	_____ in.	11.5 in.	_____ in.^{2}
9.	21 ft.	_____ ft.	_____ ft.^{2}
10.	_____ cm	30 cm	_____ cm^2

Lesson 6.6 Surface Area of a Pyramid

The **surface area (SA)** of a prism is the sum of the areas of all surfaces of the prism. The surface area of a square pyramid is the sum of the area of the square base and each of the four triangular sides.

Each triangle's area is $\frac{1}{2}$ base × height. In a pyramid, base is the side length, and height is the slant height, or length.

So, surface area (SA) = area of square base + area of four triangular sides.

$SA = (\text{side} \times \text{side}) + 4(\frac{1}{2} \text{ side} \times \text{length})$

$SA = s^2 + 2s\ell$

SA is given in square units, or units^2.

side

slant height, or length (ℓ) of the side

Find the surface area of each square pyramid.

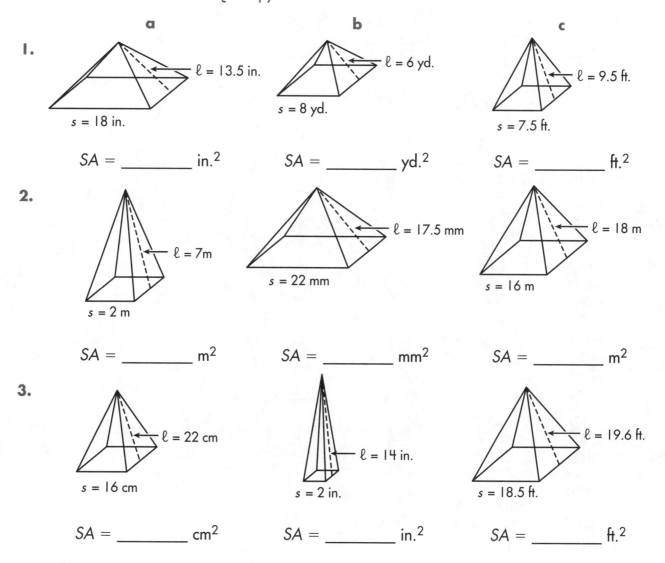

	a	b	c
1.	$\ell = 13.5$ in. $s = 18$ in.	$\ell = 6$ yd. $s = 8$ yd.	$\ell = 9.5$ ft. $s = 7.5$ ft.
	SA = _____ in.^{2}	SA = _____ yd.^{2}	SA = _____ ft.^{2}
2.	$\ell = 7$m $s = 2$ m	$\ell = 17.5$ mm $s = 22$ mm	$\ell = 18$ m $s = 16$ m
	SA = _____ m^2	SA = _____ mm^2	SA = _____ m^2
3.	$\ell = 22$ cm $s = 16$ cm	$\ell = 14$ in. $s = 2$ in.	$\ell = 19.6$ ft. $s = 18.5$ ft.
	SA = _____ cm^2	SA = _____ in.^{2}	SA = _____ ft.^{2}

Lesson 6.7 Surface Area of a Rectangular Prism

The surface area of a prism is the sum of the areas of all the faces (or surfaces) of the prism. A rectangular prism has six surfaces.

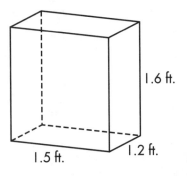

1.6 ft.

1.5 ft. 1.2 ft.

The area of each surface is determined by finding length × width, length × height, and width × height. Calculate the total surface area using the formula $SA = 2lw + 2lh + 2wh$.

In the figure on the left, $l = 1.5$ ft., $w = 1.2$ ft., and $h = 1.6$ ft.

$SA = 2(1.5 \text{ ft.})(1.2 \text{ ft.}) + 2(1.5 \text{ ft.})(1.6 \text{ ft.}) + 2(1.2 \text{ ft.})(1.6 \text{ ft.})$

$SA = 3.6 \text{ ft.}^2 + 4.8 \text{ ft.}^2 + 3.82 \text{ ft.}^2$

$SA = 12.22 \text{ ft.}^2$

Find the surface area of each figure.

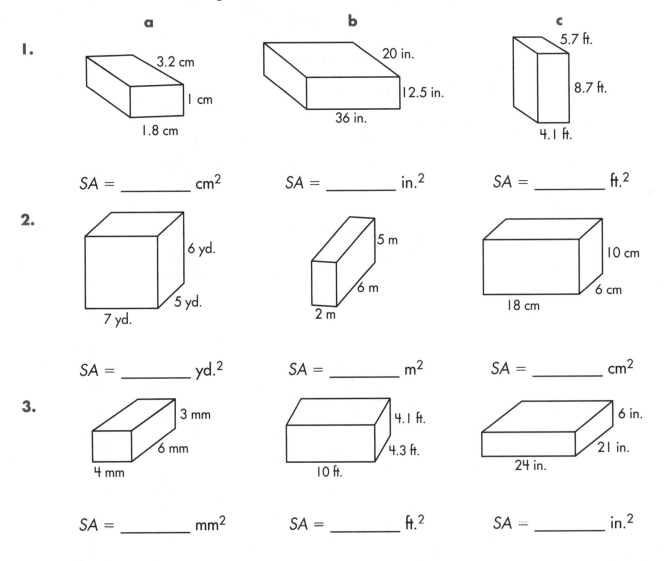

a   b   c

1.

3.2 cm
1 cm
1.8 cm

20 in.
12.5 in.
36 in.

5.7 ft.
8.7 ft.
4.1 ft.

SA = _____ cm²   SA = _____ in.²   SA = _____ ft.²

2.

6 yd.
5 yd.
7 yd.

5 m
6 m
2 m

10 cm
6 cm
18 cm

SA = _____ yd.²   SA = _____ m²   SA = _____ cm²

3.

3 mm
6 mm
4 mm

4.1 ft.
4.3 ft.
10 ft.

6 in.
21 in.
24 in.

SA = _____ mm²   SA = _____ ft.²   SA = _____ in.²

Lesson 6.8 Problem Solving

Solve each problem.

1. Mr. Ruiz's photo album is 3 inches long, 2 inches wide, and 9 inches tall. What is the surface area of the photo album?

   The surface area of the photo album is _____ square inches.

2. Andrew has a covered aquarium that is 16 inches long, 10 inches wide, and 9 inches deep. What is the surface area of Andrew's aquarium?

   The surface area of Andrew's aquarium is _____ square inches.

3. A city park is shaped like a right triangle. Its base is 20 yards and its depth is 48 yards. What is the area of the park?

   The area of the park is _____ square yards.

4. A brick is 3 inches wide, 2 inches high, and 6 inches long. What is the surface area of the brick?

   The surface area is _____ square inches.

5. A tabletop is shaped like a right triangle with a base of 25 inches and a depth of 30 inches. What is the area of the tabletop?

   The area of the tabletop is _____ square inches.

6. A rectangular playground is 90 yards long and 40 yards wide. What is the area of the playground?

   The area of the playground is _____ square yards.

	1.
	2.
	3.
	4.
	5.
	6.

Lesson 6.8 Problem Solving

Solve each problem.

1. Craig's backyard is a rectangle 25 meters long and 20 meters wide. What is the area of Craig's yard?

    The area of Craig's yard is _____ square meters.

    1.

2. A shipping crate is 0.85 meters long, 0.4 meters wide, and 0.3 meters high. What is the surface area of the crate?

    The crate's surface area is _____ square meters.

    2.

3. A rectangular poster is 45 centimeters long and 28 centimeters wide. What is the perimeter of the poster?

    The poster's perimeter is _____ centimeters.

    3.

4. A room is 8.6 meters wide and 10.2 meters long. What is the area of the room?

    The area of the room is _____ square meters.

    4.

5. Megan's jewelry box is 25 centimeters long, 12 centimeters wide, and 10 centimeters high. What is the surface area of Megan's jewelry box?

    The surface area of Megan's jewelry box is _____ square centimeters.

    5.

6. A rectangular CD jewel case is approximately 14 centimeters long and 12 centimeters wide. What is the area of the CD jewel case?

    The area of the jewel case is _____ square centimeters.

    6.

Lesson 6.9 Surface Area of a Cone

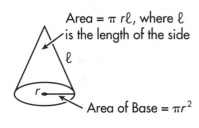

Area = π rℓ, where ℓ is the length of the side

Area of Base = πr²

The surface area (*SA*) of a cone is the sum of the area of the base plus the area of the top portion of the cone.

$$SA = \pi r\ell + \pi r^2 = \pi r(\ell + r)$$

If ℓ = 9 in. and *r* = 4 in., what is the surface area of the cone? Use 3.14 for π.

$$SA = \pi r(\ell + r) = \pi 4 \text{ in. } (9 \text{ in. } + 4 \text{ in.}) = (3.14)52 \text{ in.}^2$$
$$= 163.28 \text{ in.}^2$$

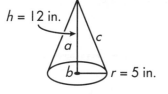

h = 12 in.

r = 5 in.

If you do not know the length of the side but do know the height of the cone, use the Pythagorean Theorem to find the length.

$$a^2 + b^2 = c^2$$
$$(12 \text{ in.})^2 + (5 \text{ in.})^2 = c^2$$
$$c^2 = 169 \text{ in.}^2$$
$$c = 13 \text{ in. } = \text{ length } (\ell)$$

Therefore, $SA = \pi r(\ell + r) = \pi 5 \text{ in. } (13 \text{ in. } + 5 \text{ in.}) = (3.14)90 \text{ in.}^2$
$$= 282.6 \text{ in.}^2$$

Find the surface area of each figure. Round to the nearest hundredth.

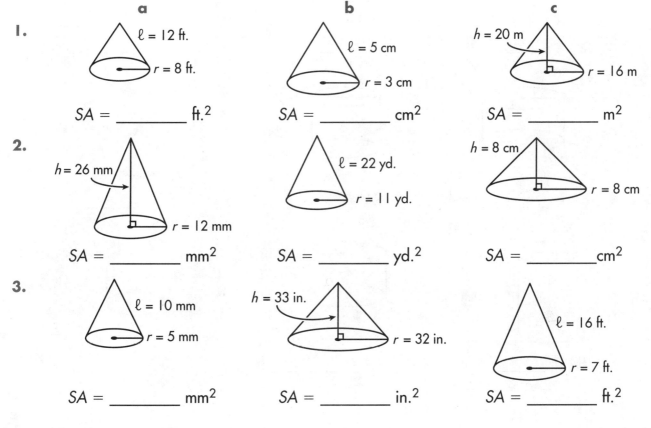

        a   **b**   **c**

1.   ℓ = 12 ft.   ℓ = 5 cm   h = 20 m
          r = 8 ft.   r = 3 cm   r = 16 m

     SA = _____ ft.²   SA = _____ cm²   SA = _____ m²

2. h = 26 mm   h = 8 cm
                            ℓ = 22 yd.
            r = 12 mm   r = 11 yd.   r = 8 cm

     SA = _____ mm²   SA = _____ yd.²   SA = _____ cm²

3.   ℓ = 10 mm   h = 33 in.
          r = 5 mm   ℓ = 16 ft.
                            r = 32 in.   r = 7 ft.

     SA = _____ mm²   SA = _____ in.²   SA = _____ ft.²

Lesson 6.10 Surface Area of a Cylinder

The surface area of a cylinder is the area of the circles plus the area of the round section in the middle. The surface area (SA) is found with the formula: $SA = 2\pi r^2 + 2\pi rh$.

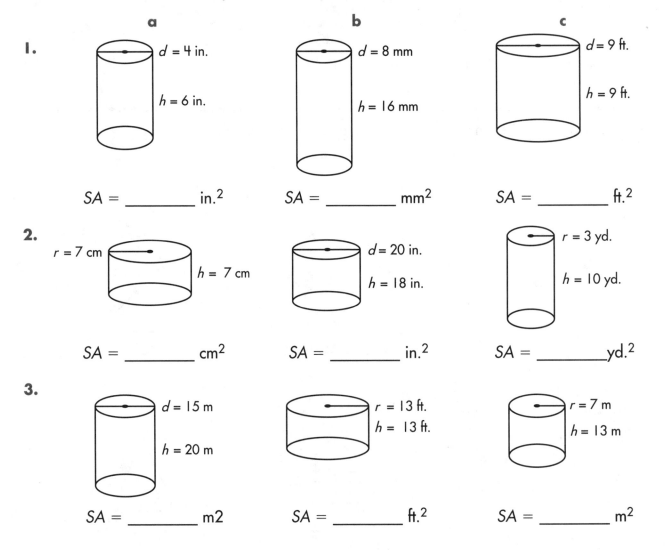

$A = \pi r^2$

$A = \text{circumference} \times \text{height} = (2\pi r) \times h$

$A = \pi r^2$

In the figure on the left, if $r = 3$ cm and $h = 8$ cm, what is the surface area? Use 3.14 for π.

$SA = 2\pi r^2 + 2\pi rh$

$\quad = 2\pi(3 \text{ cm})^2 + 2\pi(3 \text{ cm})(8 \text{ cm})$

$\quad = 3.14(18 \text{cm}^2) + 3.14(48 \text{ cm}^2)$

$\quad = 207.24 \text{ cm}^2$

Find the surface area for each cylinder. Remember that $d = 2r$.

a	b	c

1.

$d = 4$ in.

$h = 6$ in.

$SA = $ _____ in.^{2}

$d = 8$ mm

$h = 16$ mm

$SA = $ _____ mm^2

$d = 9$ ft.

$h = 9$ ft.

$SA = $ _____ ft.^{2}

2.

$r = 7$ cm

$h = 7$ cm

$SA = $ _____ cm^2

$d = 20$ in.

$h = 18$ in.

$SA = $ _____ in.^{2}

$r = 3$ yd.

$h = 10$ yd.

$SA = $ _____ yd.^{2}

3.

$d = 15$ m

$h = 20$ m

$SA = $ _____ m2

$r = 13$ ft.

$h = 13$ ft.

$SA = $ _____ ft.^{2}

$r = 7$ m

$h = 13$ m

$SA = $ _____ m^2

Lesson 6.11 Nets and Surface Area

A **net** of a three-dimensional figure shows all of the faces of the figure as one two-dimensional figure. A net of a figure can be used to find its surface area. The area of the net is equal to the surface area of the three-dimensional figure it represents.

One method to make a net is to draw a base of the three-dimensional figure. Then, surround the base by the lateral faces. If the figure is a prism, connect the other base to a face of the figure.

A second method is to draw all of the lateral faces as a single two-dimensional figure. After drawing the lateral faces, draw any bases along the correct lengths of the lateral faces.

To find the surface area of the net, add the area of each square, rectangle, triangle, or other polygon in the net.

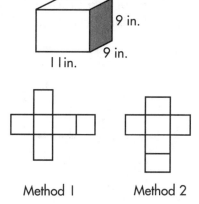

Method 1   Method 2

Draw a net for each three-dimensional figure.

a   **b**

1.

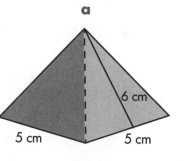

5 cm   6 cm   5 cm

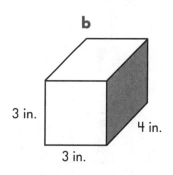

3 in.   4 in.   3 in.

2.

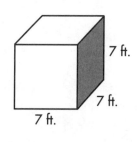

7 ft.   7 ft.   7 ft.

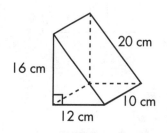

16 cm   20 cm   10 cm   12 cm

Lesson 6.11 Nets and Surface Area

Find the surface area of the three-dimensional figure represented by each net.
Draw the three-dimensional figure for each net.

1.

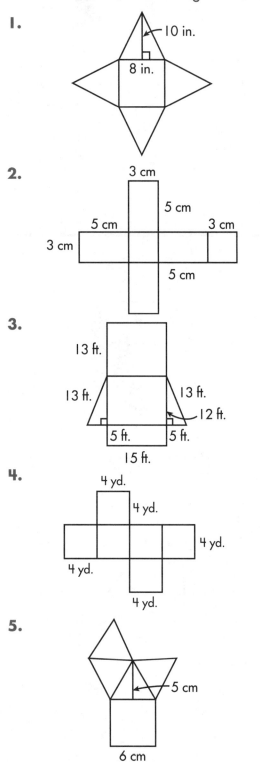

10 in.

8 in.

2.

3 cm

5 cm

5 cm   3 cm

3 cm

5 cm

3.

13 ft.

13 ft.   13 ft.

12 ft.

5 ft.   5 ft.

15 ft.

4.

4 yd.

4 yd.

4 yd.

4 yd.

4 yd.

5.

5 cm

6 cm

Lesson 6.12   Cross Sections of 3-Dimensional Figures

A cross section of a 3-dimensional figure is the place where a plane cuts through the figure. The shape and size of the cross section depends on where the plane slices the figure.

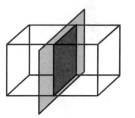

When the plane intersects a rectangular prism at a right angle, another rectangle is created.

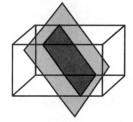

When the plane intersects a rectangular prism at an angle, it will create a quadrilateral, but not necessarily a rectangle.

Name the shape that is created by the cross section.

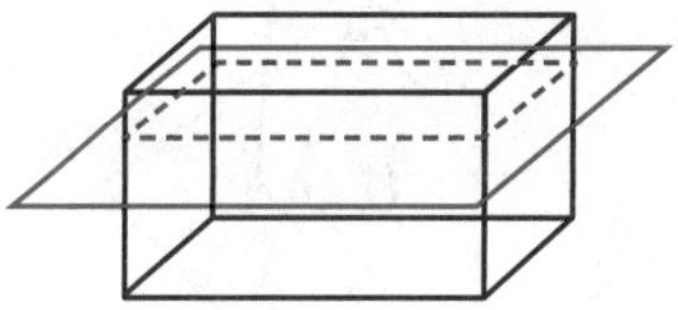

a	b

1.

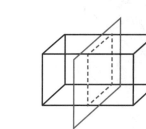   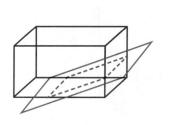

_____   _____

2.

   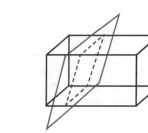

_____   _____

3.

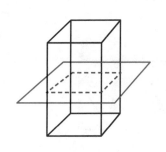   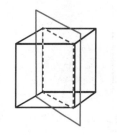

_____   _____

Lesson 6.12 Cross Sections of 3-Dimensional Figures

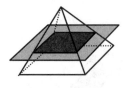

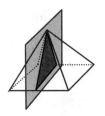

When the plane intersects a square pyramid parallel to the base, a square is created.

When the plane intersects a square pyramid through the top vertex and perpendicular to the base, a triangle is created.

When the plane intersects a square pyramid perpendicular to the base but not through the top vertex, a trapezoid is created.

Tell what shape is created by the cross section.

a   **b**

1.

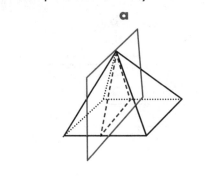

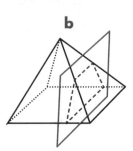

_____   _____

2.

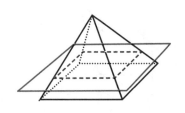

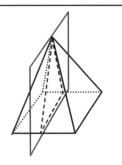

_____   _____

3.

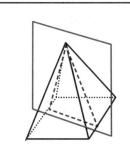

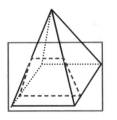

_____   _____

Lesson 6.13 Problem Solving

Solve each problem. Use 3.14 for π. When necessary, round answers to the nearest hundredth.

1. Roberto's family is putting up a backyard fence that is 75 feet long by 50 feet wide. How much fencing will Roberto's family need? How much area will Roberto have in which to play soccer?

   Roberto's family will need _____ feet of fencing.

   Roberto will have _____ square feet for soccer.

2. The students at Kennedy Middle School are painting a dunking booth for the school carnival. The booth measures 10 feet high, 8 feet wide, and 9 feet deep. How much surface area will they be painting?

   The students will be painting _____ square feet.

3. Tamara made a chocolate cake in a square baking pan. She can cut the cake into 20 pieces that measure 2 inches by 2 inches each. What is the total surface area of cake that she made? If the length of the pan is 10 inches, what is the width of the pan?

   The total surface area of the cake is _____ square inches.

   The width of the pan is _____ inches.

4. Trey drew a house for the school play, as shown on the right. The house is made up of a rectangle for the walls and a triangle for the roof. If Trey wants to paint the house, what area would he need to cover?

   The area of the house is _____ square feet.

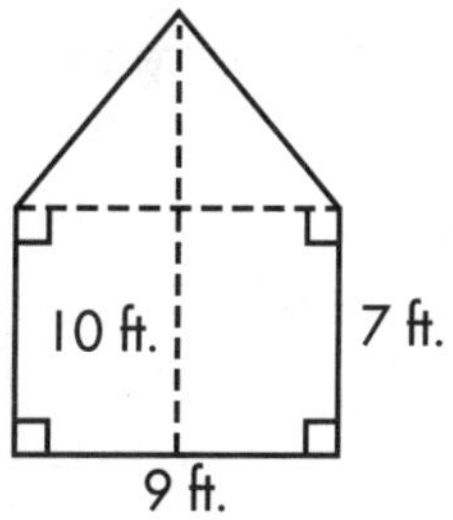

5. Shannon is sewing a round tablecloth for the kitchen table. The diameter of the table is 1.5 meters, and Shannon wants the tablecloth to hang over the edge of the table about 0.25 meter on each side. What is the total diameter of the tablecloth? What is the area of the tablecloth?

   The diameter of the tablecloth is _____ meters.

   The area of the tablecloth is _____ square meters.

Check What You Learned

Perimeter and Area

Find the perimeter of each figure.

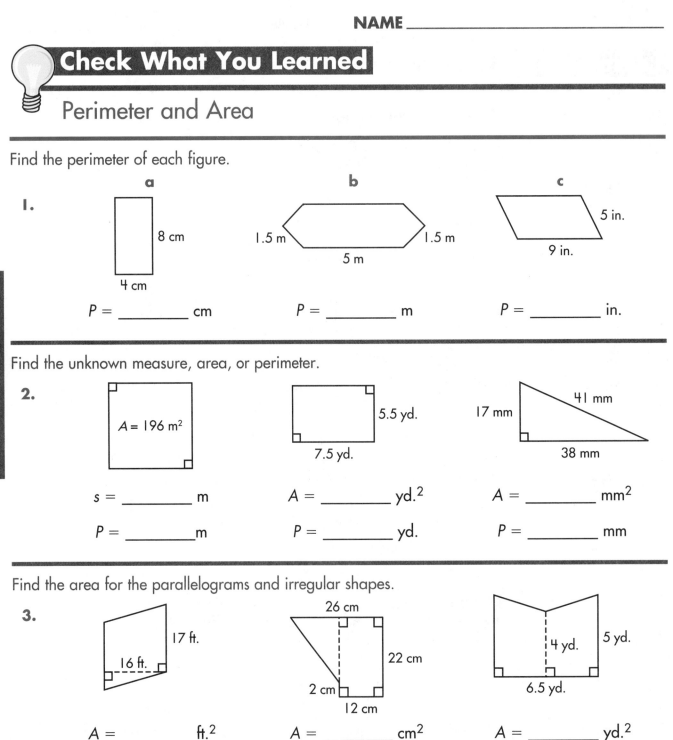

	a	b	c
1.	8 cm, 4 cm	1.5 m, 5 m, 1.5 m	5 in., 9 in.

P = _____ cm   P = _____ m   P = _____ in.

Find the unknown measure, area, or perimeter.

2.

$A = 196 \text{ m}^2$ 5.5 yd., 7.5 yd.   41 mm, 17 mm, 38 mm

s = _____ m   A = _____ yd.^{2} A = _____ mm^2

P = _____ m   P = _____ yd.   P = _____ mm

Find the area for the parallelograms and irregular shapes.

3.

17 ft., 16 ft.   26 cm, 22 cm, 2 cm, 12 cm   4 yd., 5 yd., 6.5 yd.

A = _____ ft.^{2} A = _____ cm^2 A = _____ yd.^{2}

Complete the information for each circle described below. Use 3.14 for π. When necessary, round to the nearest hundredth.

	Radius	Diameter	Area
4.	3.5 yd.	_____ yd.	_____ yd.^{2}
5.	_____ m	_____ m	201 m^2

Check What You Learned

Perimeter and Area

Find the surface area of each solid figure.

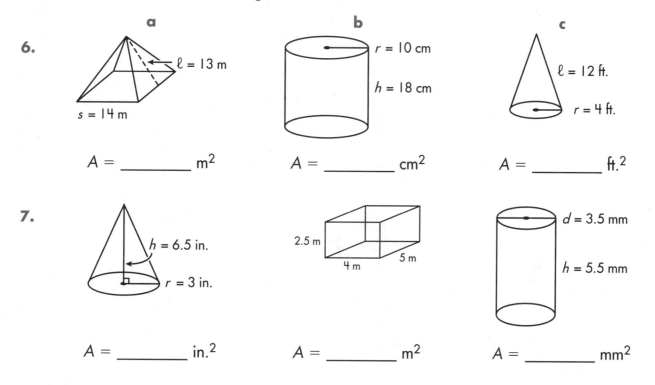

a	b	c
6. $\ell = 13$ m, $s = 14$ m	$r = 10$ cm, $h = 18$ cm	$\ell = 12$ ft., $r = 4$ ft.
A = _____ m²	A = _____ cm²	A = _____ ft.²

7. $h = 6.5$ in., $r = 3$ in. · 2.5 m, 4 m, 5 m · $d = 3.5$ mm, $h = 5.5$ mm

A = _____ in.²   A = _____ m²   A = _____ mm²

8. Hope wants to walk three times around the mall. The mall measures 2,000 feet long by 1,000 feet wide. What is the perimeter of the mall? How many total feet will Hope walk?

The perimeter of the mall is _____ feet.

Hope will walk a total of _____ feet.

9. Caleb wants to paint a model rocket for his science project. The top part of the rocket is in the shape of a cone. It has a radius of 6 inches and a length of 12 inches. The bottom part of the rocket is in the shape of a cylinder. It has a diameter of 12 inches and a height of 18 inches. What is the total surface area that Caleb must paint?

The surface area of the cone is _____ square inches.

The surface area of the cylinder is _____ square inches.

Caleb must paint a total of _____ square inches.

NAME _____

Check What You Know

Volume

Find the volume of each figure.

a	b	c

1.

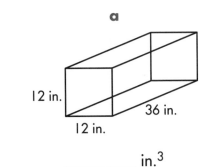

12 in.
12 in.
36 in.

_____ in.³

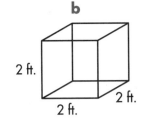

2 ft.
2 ft.
2 ft.

_____ ft.³

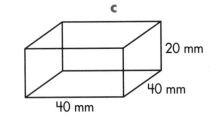

20 mm
40 mm
40 mm

_____ mm³

2.

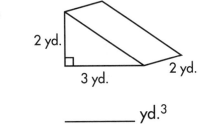
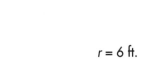

2 yd.
3 yd.
2 yd.

_____ yd.³

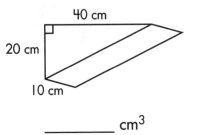

40 cm
20 cm
10 cm

_____ cm³

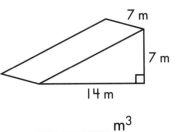

7 m
7 m
14 m

_____ m³

3.

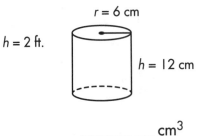

r = 6 ft.
h = 2 ft.

_____ ft.³

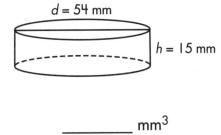

r = 6 cm
h = 12 cm

_____ cm³

d = 54 mm
h = 15 mm

_____ mm³

4.

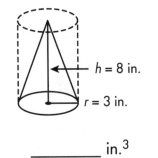

h = 8 in.
r = 3 in.

_____ in.³

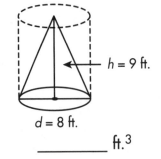

h = 9 ft.
d = 8 ft.

_____ ft.³

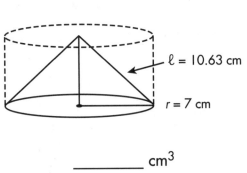

ℓ = 10.63 cm
r = 7 cm

_____ cm³

Check What You Know

Volume

Find the volume of each figure.

a	b	c

5.

$h = 2.5$ yd.

$s = 2$ yd.

_____ yd.^{3}

$\ell = 22.5$ in.

$s = 30$ in.

_____ in.^{3}

$h = 30$ cm

$s = 24$ cm

_____ cm^3

Solve each problem. Use 3.14 for π. Round answers to the nearest hundredth.

6. Jaime's water bottle has a diameter of 10 centimeters and a length of 30 centimeters. If Jaime fills the water bottle, how many cubic centimeters of water will it hold?

The water bottle's volume is _____ cubic centimeters.

7. Sonia bought a box of cat food that is 15 inches wide, 12 inches high, and 4 inches deep. How many cubic inches of cat food are in the box?

The box contains _____ cubic inches.

8. Antonio is filling paper cones with sugared almonds for the school fair. The paper cone is 7 inches deep and 3 inches in diameter at its widest. How many cubic inches of sugared almonds will each cone hold?

The cone will hold _____ cubic inches.

Lesson 7.1 Volume of Rectangular Prism

The **volume of a rectangular prism** is the product of the length times width times height. The product of the length times width is the base. The formula for the volume is $V = B \times h$. Because volume is measured in three dimensions, it is expressed in **cubic units,** or **units³**.

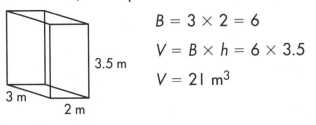

$$B = 3 \times 2 = 6$$
$$V = B \times h = 6 \times 3.5$$
$$V = 21 \text{ m}^3$$

3.5 m
3 m
2 m

Find the volume of each rectangular prism.

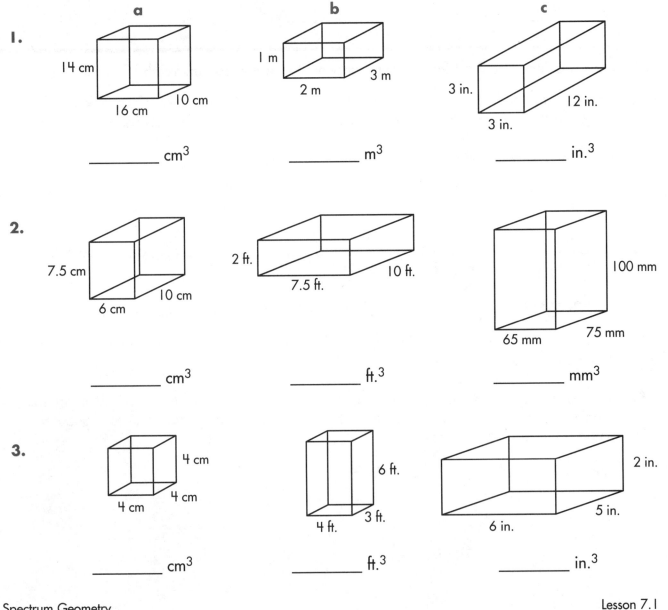

a	**b**	**c**
1. 14 cm, 16 cm, 10 cm	1 m, 2 m, 3 m	3 in., 3 in., 12 in.
_____ cm³	_____ m³	_____ in.³
2. 7.5 cm, 6 cm, 10 cm	2 ft., 7.5 ft., 10 ft.	100 mm, 65 mm, 75 mm
_____ cm³	_____ ft.³	_____ mm³
3. 4 cm, 4 cm, 4 cm	6 ft., 4 ft., 3 ft.	2 in., 6 in., 5 in.
_____ cm³	_____ ft.³	_____ in.³

Lesson 7.2 Volume of Rectangular Prisms

The volume of a rectangular prism with fractional edge lengths can also be measured by packing the prism with cubes that share a common denominator with the edge lengths. In this rectangular prism, each side length has a denominator of 5, so the prism can be packed with $\frac{1}{5}$ inch cubes to determine its volume.

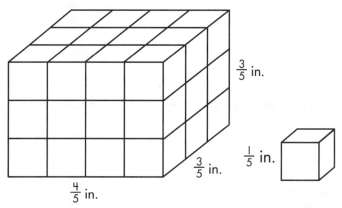

$\frac{3}{5}$ in.

$\frac{1}{5}$ in.

$\frac{3}{5}$ in.

$\frac{4}{5}$ in.

First, calculate the volume of the cube itself.

$\frac{1}{5} \times \frac{1}{5} \times \frac{1}{5} = \frac{1}{125}$ cubic inches

Next, add up the cubes in the prism. You can see from the top layer that there are 12 cubes per layer, and $12 \times 3 = 36$.

Last, multiply the number of cubes times the volume of one cube.

$36 \times \frac{1}{125} = \frac{36}{125}$ cubic inches

This is the same answer you get when you use the formula $l \times w \times h$. $\frac{4}{5} \times \frac{3}{5} \times \frac{3}{5} = \frac{36}{125}$

Find the volume of each rectangular prism. Reduce your answers.

a   b

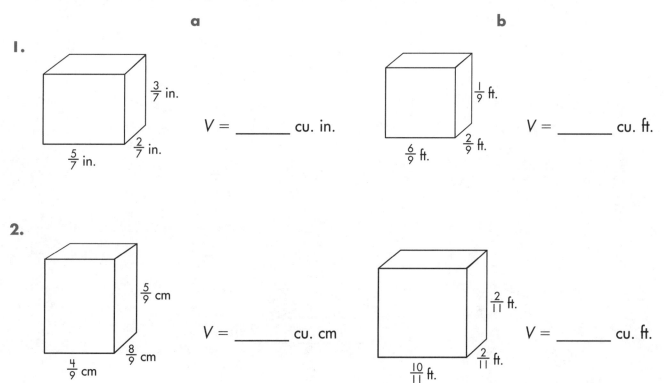

1.

$\frac{3}{7}$ in.

$\frac{2}{7}$ in.

$\frac{5}{7}$ in.

$V =$ _____ cu. in.

$\frac{1}{9}$ ft.

$\frac{2}{9}$ ft.

$\frac{6}{9}$ ft.

$V =$ _____ cu. ft.

2.

$\frac{5}{9}$ cm

$\frac{8}{9}$ cm

$\frac{4}{9}$ cm

$V =$ _____ cu. cm

$\frac{2}{11}$ ft.

$\frac{2}{11}$ ft.

$\frac{10}{11}$ ft.

$V =$ _____ cu. ft.

Lesson 7.3 Volume of Triangular Prisms

The **volume of a triangular prism** is the product of the area of the base (*B*) times the height. The base of a triangular prism is a triangle. To find the volume, multiply the area of one base times the height. Volume is expressed in **cubic units**, or **units³**.

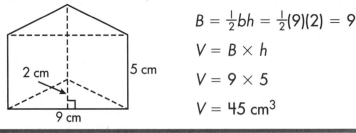

$B = \frac{1}{2}bh = \frac{1}{2}(9)(2) = 9$

$V = B \times h$

$V = 9 \times 5$

$V = 45 \text{ cm}^3$

Find the volume of each figure.

| a | b | c |

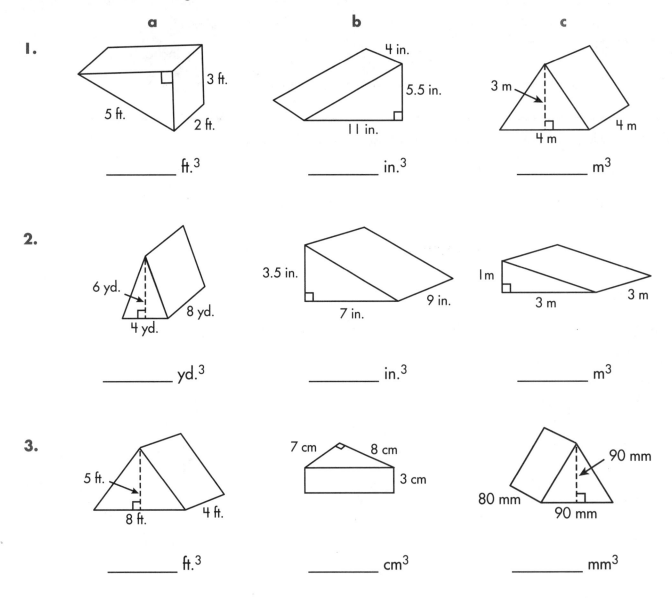

1.

a. _____ ft.³

b. _____ in.³

c. _____ m³

2.

_____ yd.³

_____ in.³

_____ m³

3.

_____ ft.³

_____ cm³

_____ mm³

Lesson 7.4   Volume of a Cylinder

The **volume of a cylinder** is the product of the area of the base *(B)* times the height. The formula for the volume of a cylinder is $V = B \times h$. Volume is expressed in **cubic units**, or **units^3**.

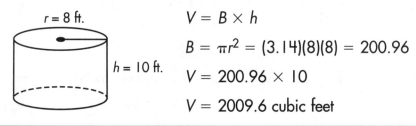

$V = B \times h$

$B = \pi r^2 = (3.14)(8)(8) = 200.96$

$V = 200.96 \times 10$

$V = 2009.6$ cubic feet

Find the volume of each figure. Round answers to the nearest hundredth. Remember, $d = 2r$.

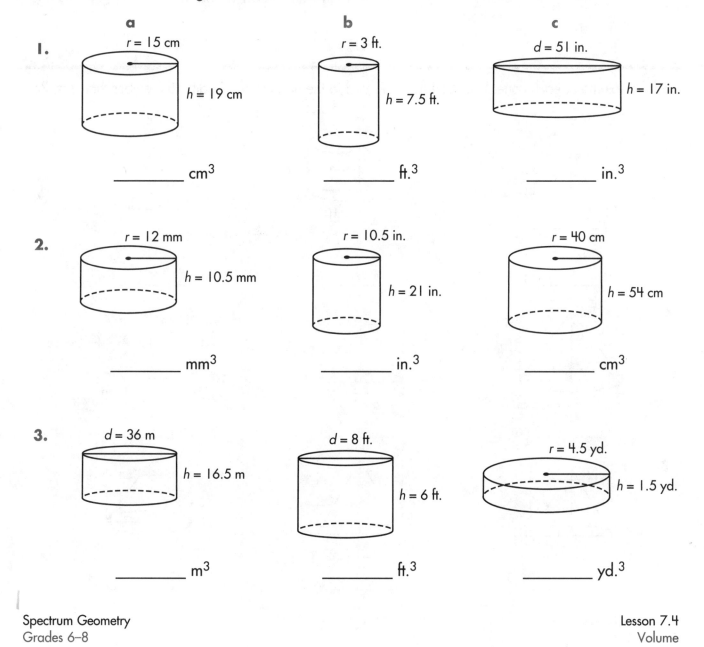

	a	b	c
1.	$r = 15$ cm $h = 19$ cm	$r = 3$ ft. $h = 7.5$ ft.	$d = 51$ in. $h = 17$ in.
	_____ cm^3	_____ ft.^{3}	_____ in.^{3}
2.	$r = 12$ mm $h = 10.5$ mm	$r = 10.5$ in. $h = 21$ in.	$r = 40$ cm $h = 54$ cm
	_____ mm^3	_____ in.^{3}	_____ cm^3
3.	$d = 36$ m $h = 16.5$ m	$d = 8$ ft. $h = 6$ ft.	$r = 4.5$ yd. $h = 1.5$ yd.
	_____ m^3	_____ ft.^{3}	_____ yd.^{3}

Lesson 7.5 Volume of a Cone

The **volume of a cone** is calculated as $\frac{1}{3}$ base × height. This is because a cone occupies $\frac{1}{3}$ of the volume of a cylinder of the same height.

Base is the area of the circle, πr^2. Volume is given in **cubic units**, or **units³**.

$$V = \frac{1}{3}\pi r^2 h$$

If the height of a cone is 7 cm and radius is 3 cm, what is the volume?

Use 3.14 for π. $V = \frac{1}{3}\pi 3^2 7$ $V = \pi\frac{63}{3}$ $V = p\ 21$ $V = 65.94$ cm³

If you do not know the height but you do know the radius and the length of the side, you can use the Pythagorean Theorem ($a^2 + b^2 = c^2$) to find the height. In this case, $b = 12$.

$$V = \frac{1}{3}\pi r^2 h = \frac{1}{3}\pi \times 81 \times 12 = 324\pi = 1017.36 \text{ m}^3$$

Find the volume of each cone. Use 3.14 for π. Round to the nearest hundredth. Remember that $d = 2r$.

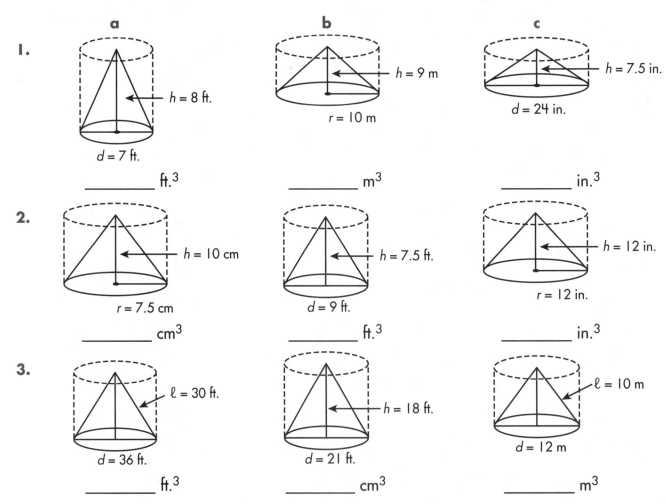

a

b

c

1.

$h = 8$ ft.

$d = 7$ ft.

_____ ft.³

$h = 9$ m

$r = 10$ m

_____ m³

$h = 7.5$ in.

$d = 24$ in.

_____ in.³

2.

$h = 10$ cm

$r = 7.5$ cm

_____ cm³

$h = 7.5$ ft.

$d = 9$ ft.

_____ ft.³

$h = 12$ in.

$r = 12$ in.

_____ in.³

3.

$\ell = 30$ ft.

$d = 36$ ft.

_____ ft.³

$h = 18$ ft.

$d = 21$ ft.

_____ cm³

$\ell = 10$ m

$d = 12$ m

_____ m³

Lesson 7.6 Volume of a Pyramid

The volume of a pyramid is calculated as $\frac{1}{3}$ base × height. This is because a pyramid occupies $\frac{1}{3}$ of the volume of a rectangular prism of the same height.

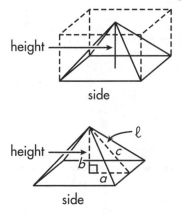

height ——

side

Because the base of a square pyramid is square, $B = s^2$.

So, $V = \frac{1}{3}Bh$ or $\frac{1}{3}s^2h$. Volume is given in **cubic units**, or **units³**.

If $s = 10$ cm and $h = 9$ cm, what is the volume?

$V = \frac{1}{3}s^2h$ $V = \frac{1}{3}10^2 \times 9$ $V = \frac{900}{3}$ $V = 300$ cm^3

height ——

side

If you do not know the height but you do know the slant height or length of the side, you can use the Pythagorean Theorem to find the height.

$a = \frac{1}{2}$ of the side length, $b =$ the height of the pyramid, $c =$ length

If $s = 6$ m and $l = 5$ m, what is h? $a^2 + b^2 = c^2$ $3^2 + b^2 = 25$ m $b^2 = 16$ $b = 4$ m

Find the volume of each pyramid. Round answers to the nearest hundredth.

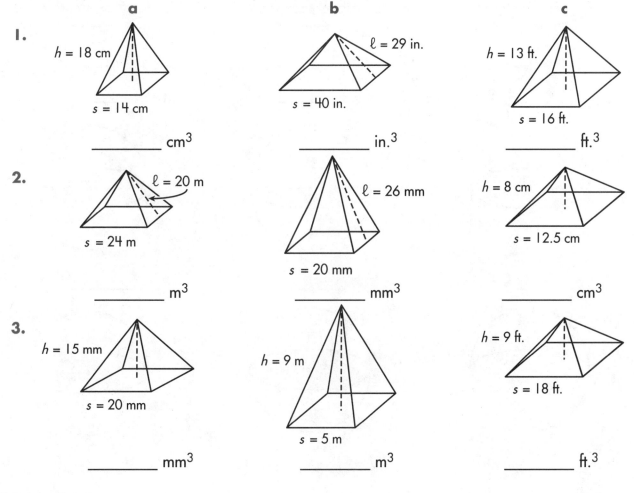

	a	b	c
1.	$h = 18$ cm, $s = 14$ cm	$l = 29$ in., $s = 40$ in.	$h = 13$ ft., $s = 16$ ft.
	_____ cm^3	_____ in.^{3}	_____ ft.^{3}
2.	$l = 20$ m, $s = 24$ m	$l = 26$ mm, $s = 20$ mm	$h = 8$ cm, $s = 12.5$ cm
	_____ m^3	_____ mm^3	_____ cm^3
3.	$h = 15$ mm, $s = 20$ mm	$h = 9$ m, $s = 5$ m	$h = 9$ ft., $s = 18$ ft.
	_____ mm^3	_____ m^3	_____ ft.^{3}

Lesson 7.7 Volume of a Sphere

Volume is the amount of space a three-dimensional figure occupies. The **volume of a sphere** is calculated as $V = \frac{4}{3}\pi r^3$. When the diameter of a sphere is known, it can be divided by 2 and then the formula for the volume of a sphere can be used.

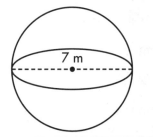

$V = \frac{4}{3}\pi r^3$ Volume is given in **cubic units** or **units³**.

The radius of a sphere is half of its diameter. Find the radius, then calculate the volume.

$r = \frac{1}{2}d = \frac{1}{2}(7) = \frac{7}{2} = 3.5$

$V = \frac{4}{3}\pi(3.5)3 = \frac{4}{3}\pi(42.875) = 179.5$ cubic meters

Find the volume of each sphere. Use 3.14 to represent π. Round answers to the nearest hundredth.

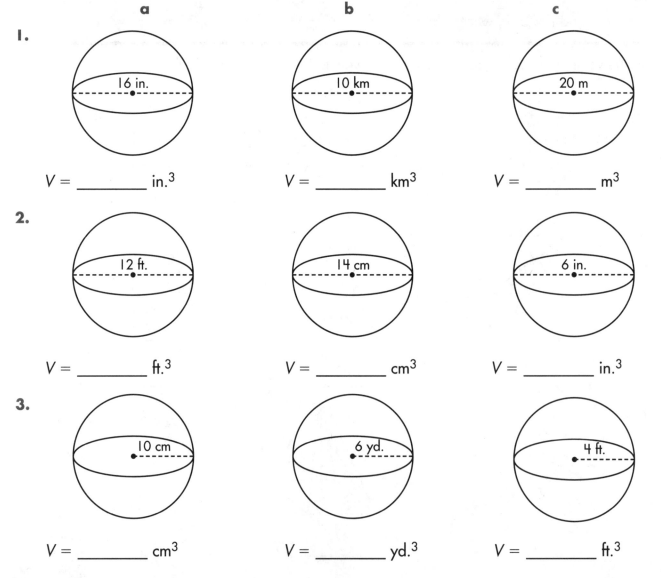

a

b

c

1.

16 in.

V = _____ in.³

10 km

V = _____ km³

20 m

V = _____ m³

2.

12 ft.

V = _____ ft.³

14 cm

V = _____ cm³

6 in.

V = _____ in.³

3.

10 cm

V = _____ cm³

6 yd.

V = _____ yd.³

4 ft.

V = _____ ft.³

Lesson 7.8 Problem Solving with Volume

SHOW YOUR WORK

Solve each problem. Use 3.14 for π. Round answers to the nearest hundredth.

1. Jermaine has a mailing cylinder for posters that measures 18 inches long and 6 inches in diameter. What volume can it hold?

   The cylinder can hold _____ cubic inches.

   1.

2. An oatmeal container is a cylinder measuring 16 centimeters in diameter and 32 centimeters tall. How much oatmeal can the container hold?

   The container can hold _____
   cubic centimeters of oatmeal.

   2.

3. Trina is using 2 glasses in an experiment. Glass A measures 8 centimeters in diameter and 18 centimeters tall. Glass B measures 10 centimeters in diameter and 13 centimeters tall. Which one can hold more liquid? How much more?

   Glass _____ can hold _____
   more cubic centimeters of liquid.

   3.

4. Paul completely filled a glass with water. The glass was 10 centimeters in diameter and 17 centimeters tall. He drank the water. What volume of water did he drink?

   Paul drank _____ cubic centimeters of water.

   4.

5. An ice-cream cone has a height of 6 inches and a diameter of 3 inches. How much ice cream can this cone hold?

   The cone can hold _____ cubic inches
   of ice cream.

   5.

6. A beach ball that is 10 inches in diameter must be inflated. How much air will it take to fill the ball?

   It will take _____ cubic inches of air to fill
   the ball.

   6.

Lesson 7.9 Problem Solving

Solve each problem. Use 3.14 for π. Round answers to the nearest hundredth.

1. Aishani bought a chicken salad wrap in the shape of a cylinder, which was 15 centimeters long and had a radius of 7 centimeters. How many cubic centimeters of chicken salad did Aishani eat if she ate half of the wrap?

    Aishani ate _____ cm^3.

2. Maddie is making soap for her sister's birthday present. She is using a tray soap mold that makes four rectangular bars at a time. Each finished bar measures 2 inches wide, 3 inches long, and 1 inch deep. If Maddie makes one tray of soap, how much does she need to fill the tray?

    Maddie needs to melt _____ in.^{3}.

3. Quon bought a wheel of brie cheese for his party. The cheese is 5 inches in diameter and $1\frac{1}{2}$ inches high. How many cubic inches of cheese are in the wheel Quon bought?

    The wheel of cheese contains _____ in.^{3}.

4. Marcus is making cupcakes for his daughter's birthday. His cupcake pan has recesses that are 6 centimeters in diameter and 4 centimeters deep. Marcus needs to fill each recess half-way. How many cubic centimeters of cake batter will each recess hold if Marcus fills it half-way? How many cubic centimeters of cake batter does Marcus need in order to make 12 cupcakes?

    The cake batter needed to make one cupcake is _____ cm^3.

    The cake batter needed to make twelve cupcakes is _____ cm^3.

Check What You Learned

Volume

Find the volume of each figure.

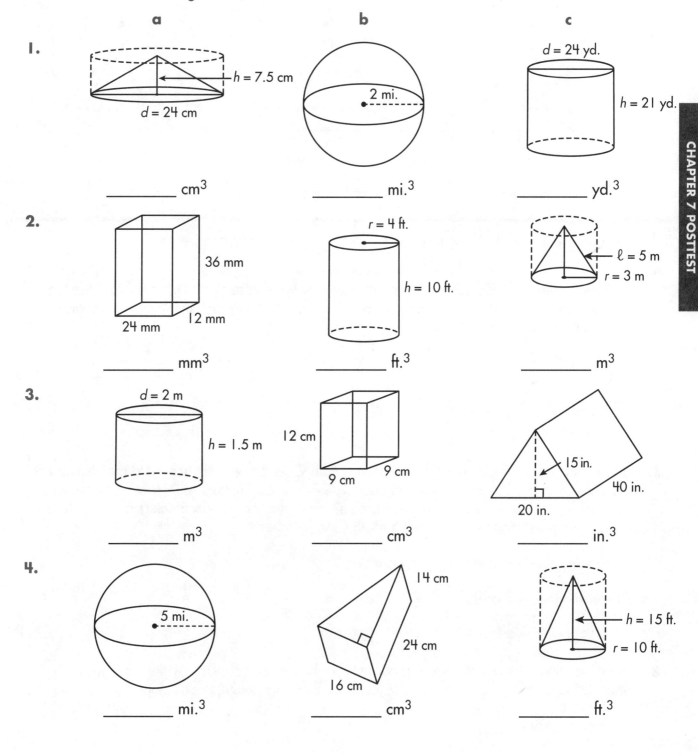

a	b	c

1.

_h_ = 7.5 cm

_d_ = 24 cm

2 mi.

_d_ = 24 yd.

_h_ = 21 yd.

_____ cm³   _____ mi.³   _____ yd.³

2.

36 mm

12 mm

24 mm

_r_ = 4 ft.

_h_ = 10 ft.

_ℓ_ = 5 m

_r_ = 3 m

_____ mm³   _____ ft.³   _____ m³

3.

_d_ = 2 m

_h_ = 1.5 m

12 cm

9 cm

9 cm

15 in.

40 in.

20 in.

_____ m³   _____ cm³   _____ in.³

4.

5 mi.

14 cm

24 cm

16 cm

_h_ = 15 ft.

_r_ = 10 ft.

_____ mi.³   _____ cm³   _____ ft.³

Check What You Learned

Volume

Find the volume of each figure.

| a | b | c |

5.

h = 20 in.
s = 16 in.

_____ in.^{3}

ℓ = 1.5 m
s = 2 m

_____ m^3

ℓ = 39 in.
s = 30 in.

_____ in.^{3}

Solve each problem. Use 3.14 for π. Round answers to the nearest hundredth.

6. Ayesha is making salsa. She will be making enough salsa to fill 6 jars that are 3.2 inches in diameter and 5.5 inches tall. If she fills each jar with salsa up to 0.5 inch from the top of the jar, how many cubic inches does each jar contain? How many cubic inches of salsa will Ayesha prepare to make 6 jars of salsa?

One jar will contain _____ in.^{3}.

Six jars will contain _____ in.^{3}.

7. Han is making pyramid-shaped rice for the Math Club dinner. His rice mold makes square pyramids that are 7.5 centimeters on each side and 7 centimeters tall. How many cubic centimeters of rice will each pyramid contain? How many cubic centimeters of rice will Han need to prepare in order to serve 15 Math Club members?

One serving will contain _____ cm^3.

Fifteen servings will contain _____ cm^3.

8. Hope has filled a box with packing peanuts. If the box is 18 inches wide, 18 inches long, and 18 inches high, how many cubic inches of packing peanuts does Hope have?

The box contains _____ in.^{3}.

Final Test Chapters 1-7

Use the figure to complete the following.

1. Name an angle that is vertical to ∠FIG. _____

2. Is ∠EJD an acute angle, an obtuse angle, or a right angle?

_____

3. Name an angle that is complementary to ∠HIA. _____

4. Name the transversal of $\overleftrightarrow{FB}$ and $\overleftrightarrow{EC}$. _____

5. What is a corresponding angle to ∠GIB. _____

Write a proportion for each problem. Then, solve the problem.

6. According to the map, a hiking trail is 12 centimeters long. If the map scale is 1 cm = 1.25 mi., how long is the trail?

The trail is _____ miles long.

7. The petting zoo has three rabbits for every two goats. If there are 18 rabbits in the zoo, how many goats are there?

The zoo has _____ goats.

Check that the triangles are proportional. Circle *similar* or *not similar*.

8. $\dfrac{AB}{DE} =$ _____ = _____

$\dfrac{BC}{EF} =$ _____ = _____

$\dfrac{AC}{DF} =$ _____ = _____

similar   not similar

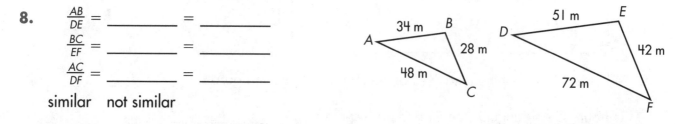

Find the length of the missing side for each pair of similar triangles. Label the side with its length.

a   **b**

9.

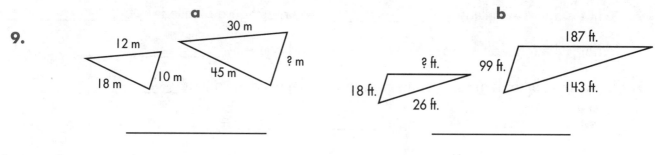

_____   _____

Final Test Chapters 1–7

Write an equation for the problem. Then, solve.

10. An angle is 65 degrees less than its supplement. Find the measure of each angle.

_____

The angles measure _____ degrees and _____ degrees.

Find the lengths of the missing sides for the right triangles using the Pythagorean Theorem. Round your answers to the nearest hundredth.

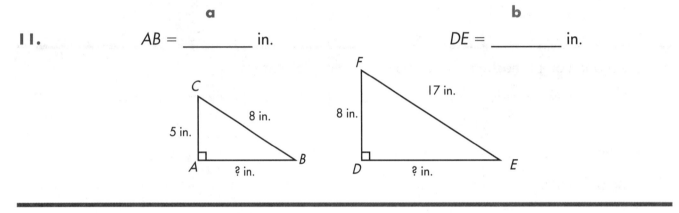

a	**b**
11. AB = _____ in.	DE = _____ in.

Use the figures to answer the questions.

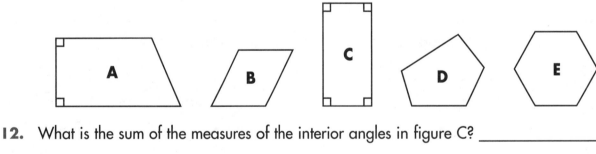

12. What is the sum of the measures of the interior angles in figure C? _____°

Is figure C equiangular, equilateral, or regular? _____

13. Is figure D convex or concave? _____

14. What is figure A called? _____ What is figure B called? _____

What is the main difference between figure A and figure B? _____

15. In figure E, what is the sum of the measures of the interior angles? _____°

What is the measure of each angle? _____°

Final Test Chapters 1–7

Solve.

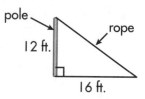

16. Campers attached a rope to a pole 12 ft. high. They pulled it tight and staked it to the ground 16 ft. from the pole. How long is the rope? _____

Plot the following coordinates on the grid and connect the points by straight lines to make the two shapes.

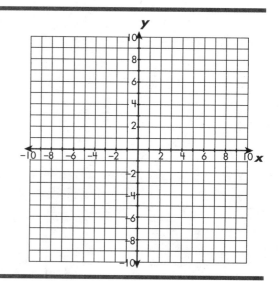

17. Shape 1: A(3, 3), B(6, 6), C(10, 6), D(7, 3)

Shape 2: E(3, −3), F(7, −3), G(10, −6), H(6, −6)

18. What type of polygon did you draw? _____

19. Is the transformation shown in the grid a translation, rotation, reflection, or dilation?

_____

Use the figure at the right to answer the questions.

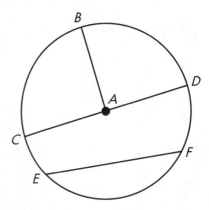

20. Name the circle. _____

21. Name the origin. _____

22. Name a radius. _____

23. Name a chord. _____

24. Name the diameter. _____

Complete the information for each circle described below. Use 3.14 for π. When necessary, round to the nearest hundredth.

	a Diameter	b Radius	c Circumference	d Area
25.	_____ cm	_____ cm	31.4 cm	_____ cm²
26.	42 in.	_____ in.	_____ in.	_____ in.²
27.	_____ ft.	9 ft.	_____ ft.	_____ ft.²

Final Test Chapters 1–7

Find the unknown measure of each shape.

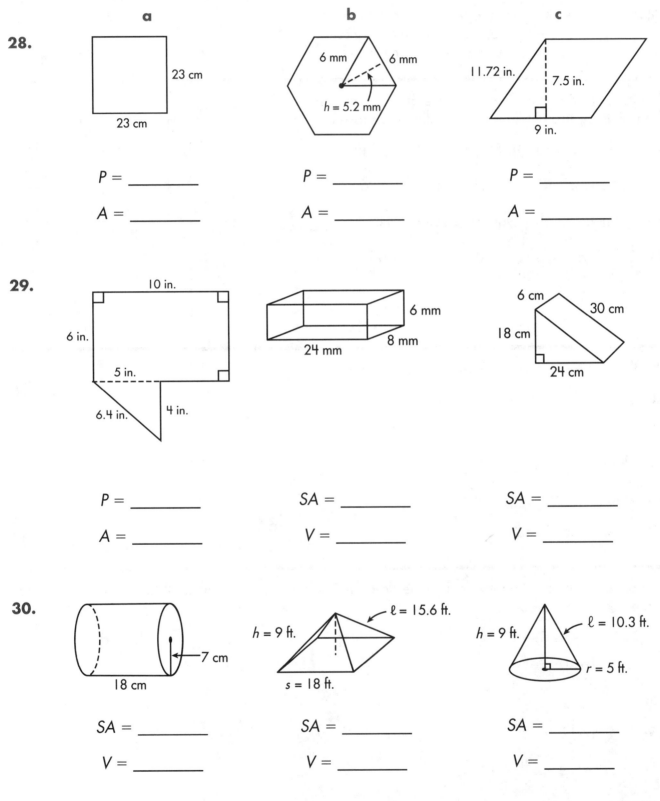

	a	**b**	**c**

28.

a: 23 cm, 23 cm

P = _____   A = _____

b: 6 mm, 6 mm, h = 5.2 mm

P = _____   A = _____

c: 11.72 in., 7.5 in., 9 in.

P = _____   A = _____

29.

a: 10 in., 6 in., 5 in., 6.4 in., 4 in.

P = _____   A = _____

b: 6 mm, 8 mm, 24 mm

SA = _____   V = _____

c: 6 cm, 30 cm, 18 cm, 24 cm

SA = _____   V = _____

30.

a: 7 cm, 18 cm

SA = _____   V = _____

b: ℓ = 15.6 ft., h = 9 ft., s = 18 ft.

SA = _____   V = _____

c: ℓ = 10.3 ft., h = 9 ft., r = 5 ft.

SA = _____   V = _____

Geometry Reference Chart

Formulas	
Perimeter of a rectangle	$P = 2l + 2w$
Area of a rectangle	$A = lw$
Perimeter of a square	$P = 4s$
Area of a square	$A = s \times s$
Perimeter of a triangle	$P = a + b + c$
Area of a triangle	$A = \frac{1}{2}bh$
Area of a circle	$A = \pi r^2$
Circumference of a circle	$C = 2\pi r$
Area of a parallelogram	$A = bh$
Surface area of a rectangular prism	$SA = 2lw + 2lh + 2wh$
Surface area of a cylinder	$SA = 2\pi r^2 + 2\pi rh$
Surface area of a cone	$SA = \pi r\ell + \pi r^2$
Surface area of a pyramid	$SA = s^2 + 2s\ell$
Volume of a rectangular prism	$V = lwh$
Volume of a triangular prism	$V = Bh$
Volume of a cylinder	$V = \pi r^2 h$
Volume of a cone	$V = \frac{1}{3}\pi r^2 h$
Volume of a pyramid	$V = \frac{1}{3}Bh$
Volume of a sphere	$V = \frac{4}{3}\pi r^3$

Pythagorean Theorem

$$a^2 + b^2 = c^2$$

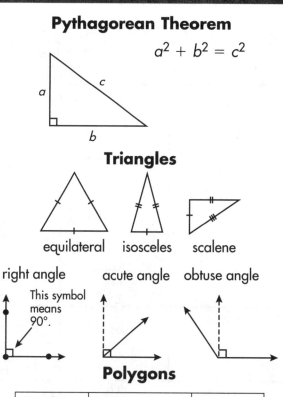

Triangles

equilateral   isosceles   scalene

right angle   acute angle   obtuse angle

This symbol means 90°.

Polygons

Prefix	Name	Sides
tri-	triangle	3
quadri-	quadrilateral	4
penta-	pentagon	5
hexa-	hexagon	6
hepta-	heptagon	7
octa-	octagon	8
nona-	nonagon	9
deca-	decagon	10

Quadrilaterals

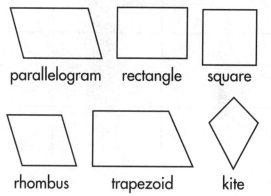

parallelogram   rectangle   square

rhombus   trapezoid   kite

Table of Squares and Square Roots

Except in the case of perfect squares, square roots shown on the chart are not exact.

Table of Squares and Square Roots					
n	n^2	$\sqrt{n}$	n	n^2	$\sqrt{n}$
1	1	1	51	2,601	7.14
2	4	1.41	52	2,704	7.21
3	9	1.73	53	2,809	7.28
4	16	2	54	2,916	7.35
5	25	2.24	55	3,025	7.42
6	36	2.45	56	3,136	7.48
7	49	2.65	57	3,249	7.55
8	64	2.83	58	3,364	7.62
9	81	3	59	3,481	7.68
10	100	3.16	60	3,600	7.75
11	121	3.32	61	3,721	7.81
12	144	3.46	62	3,844	7.87
13	169	3.61	63	3,969	7.94
14	196	3.74	64	4,096	8
15	225	3.87	65	4,225	8.06
16	256	4	66	4,356	8.12
17	289	4.12	67	4,489	8.19
18	324	4.24	68	4,624	8.25
19	361	4.36	69	4,761	8.31
20	400	4.47	70	4,900	8.37
21	441	4.58	71	5,041	8.43
22	484	4.69	72	5,184	8.49
23	529	4.80	73	5,329	8.54
24	576	4.90	74	5,476	8.60
25	625	5	75	5,625	8.66
26	676	5.10	76	5,776	8.72
27	729	5.20	77	5,929	8.77
28	784	5.29	78	6,084	8.83
29	841	5.39	79	6,241	8.89
30	900	5.48	80	6,400	8.94
31	961	5.57	81	6,561	9
32	1,024	5.66	82	6,724	9.06
33	1,089	5.74	83	6,889	9.11
34	1,156	5.83	84	7,056	9.17
35	1,225	5.92	85	7,225	9.22
36	1,296	6	86	7,396	9.27
37	1,369	6.08	87	7,569	9.33
38	1,444	6.16	88	7,744	9.38
39	1,521	6.24	89	7,921	9.43
40	1,600	6.32	90	8,100	9.49
41	1,681	6.40	91	8,281	9.54
42	1,764	6.48	92	8,464	9.59
43	1,849	6.56	93	8,649	9.64
44	1,936	6.63	94	8,836	9.70
45	2,025	6.71	95	9,025	9.75
46	2,116	6.78	96	9,216	9.80
47	2,209	6.86	97	9,409	9.85
48	2,304	6.93	98	9,604	9.90
49	2,401	7	99	9,801	9.95
50	2,500	7.07	100	10,000	10

Scoring Record for Posttests, Mid-Test, and Final Test

Chapter Posttest	Your Score	Performance			
		Excellent	Very Good	Fair	Needs Improvement
1	____ of 11	11	10	9	8 or fewer
2	____ of 20	19–20	17–18	15–16	14 or fewer
3	____ of 17	16–17	14–15	12–13	11 or fewer
4	____ of 32	29–32	26–28	23–25	22 or fewer
5	____ of 21	20–21	18–19	16–17	15 or fewer
6	____ of 19	18–19	16–17	14–15	13 or fewer
7	____ of 18	17–18	15–16	13–14	12 or fewer
Mid-Test	____ of 35	32–35	29–31	25–28	24 or fewer
Final Test	____ of 44	40–44	36–39	31–35	30 or fewer

Record your test score in the Your Score column. See where your score falls in the Performance columns. Your score is based on the total number of required responses. If your score is fair or needs improvement, review the chapter material.

Geometry Answers

Chapter 1

Check What You Know, page 1

	a	b	c
1.	line segment; $\overline{KJ}$, $\overline{JK}$, KJ	line; $\overleftrightarrow{FR}$, $\overleftrightarrow{RF}$, $\overrightarrow{FR}$	ray; PQ, $\overrightarrow{PQ}$

2. ABC, FBG, DBE, GBF
3. ∠4 (∠KLM), ∠5 (∠NLM), ∠KLM
4. ∠NLM, ∠MLN
5. 90°, right   130°, obtuse   80°, acute

Lesson 1.1, page 2

	a	b	c
1.	AB; BA	$\overleftrightarrow{AB}$; $\overleftrightarrow{BA}$	
2.	CD; DC	$\overleftrightarrow{CD}$; $\overleftrightarrow{DC}$	
3.	EF; FE	$\overleftrightarrow{EF}$; $\overleftrightarrow{FE}$	
4.	HG	$\overrightarrow{HG}$;	G; H
5.	KJ	$\overrightarrow{KJ}$;	J; K

6.
7.

Lesson 1.1, page 3

1. MKN; JKL
2. ABC; BDG, ADE
3. $\overleftrightarrow{LM}$; $\overleftrightarrow{ML}$
4. Any of the following: $\overline{ON}$; $\overline{NO}$

Lesson 1.2, page 4

	a	b
1.	CD, $\overrightarrow{CD}$	C
2.	EF, $\overrightarrow{EF}$	E
3.	GH, $\overrightarrow{GH}$	G
4.	∠IJK, ∠KJI, ∠J	
5.	∠LMN, ∠NML, ∠M	

Lesson 1.3, page 5

	a	b
1.	120°; obtuse	60°; acute
2.	90°; right	30°; acute

Lesson 1.4, page 6

1. vertical
2. supplementary
3. supplementary
4. vertical
5. vertical
6. supplementary
7. 72°
8. 68°
9. 37°
10. 60°

Lesson 1.5, page 7

1. ∠1/∠2, ∠3/∠4, ∠5/∠6, ∠7/∠8
   ∠1/∠3, ∠2/∠4, ∠5/∠7, ∠6/∠8
2. ∠4/∠5
3. ∠2/∠7
4. ∠4/∠5, ∠6/∠7, ∠8/∠9, ∠10/∠11
   ∠5/∠7, ∠4/∠6, ∠9/∠11, ∠8/∠10
5. ∠9/∠6, ∠7/∠8
6. ∠11/∠4, ∠5/∠10

Check What You Learned, page 8

1. ∠GJF
2. ∠ICD
3. ∠ACG or ∠BCJ or ∠DCI
4. 45°
5. ∠ECJ
6. ∠2/∠7; ∠3/∠6
7. ∠1/∠8; ∠4/∠5
8. 40°
9. $\overleftrightarrow{GH}$
10. 30°
11. 150°

Chapter 2

Check What You Know, page 9

	a	b	c
1.	15	8	22
2.	8	9	8
3.	4	5	4
4.	$\sqrt{3,600}$; 60		
5.	$\sqrt{19,296}$; 138.91		
6.	$\sqrt{8,955}$; 94.63		
7.	20 ft.		
8.	40	144	108

Lesson 2.1, page 10

	a	b	c
1.	acute	obtuse	right
2.	40°; obtuse	40°; acute	90°, 35°; right

Lesson 2.2, page 11

	a	b	c
1.	equilateral	scalene	isosceles
2.	equilateral	isosceles	equilateral

Lesson 2.3, page 12

Use a protractor and ruler to check the accuracy of the drawings.

Lesson 2.3, page 13

Use a protractor and ruler to check the accuracy of the drawings.

Geometry Answers

Lesson 2.3, page 14

	a	b	c
1.	no	yes	yes
2.	no	no	yes
3.	yes	yes	no
4.	no	yes	yes

Lesson 2.4, page 15

1. $\frac{15}{30} = \frac{1}{2}; \frac{15}{30} = \frac{1}{2}; \frac{12}{24} = \frac{1}{2};$ similar
2. $\frac{25}{100} = \frac{1}{4}; \frac{60}{240} = \frac{1}{4}; \frac{80}{320} = \frac{1}{4};$ similar
3. $\frac{44}{88} = \frac{1}{2}; \frac{50}{100} = \frac{1}{2}; \frac{88}{168} = \frac{11}{21};$ not similar

Lesson 2.4, page 16

	a	b
1.	36 m	14 yd.
2.	384 in.	9 m
3.	175 cm	76 ft.

Lesson 2.5, page 17

	a	b	c
1.	$6 = 6$; T	$50 \neq 24$	$9 = 9$; T
2.	$16 \neq 81$	$18 = 18$; T	$24 \neq 25$
3.	$44 = 44$; T	$36 \neq 21$	$126 = 126$; T
4.	$9 \neq 12$	$60 = 60$; T	$36 \neq 48$
5.	$360 = 360$; T	$72 = 72$; T	$26 = 26$; T
6.	$42 \neq 36$	$35 \neq 33$	$12 \neq 48$
7.	$175 = 175$; T	$144 = 144$; T	$72 \neq 84$

Lesson 2.6, page 18

	a	b	c
1.	12	12	63
2.	20	9	60
3.	1	3	2

4. $\frac{1}{15} = \frac{5}{n}$; 75 oz.
5. $\frac{5}{1000} = \frac{n}{100,000}$; $500

Lesson 2.7, page 19

1. $\frac{1}{11} = \frac{20}{n}$; 220 mi.
2. $\frac{1}{5} = \frac{n}{305}$; 61 in.
3. $\frac{6}{24} = \frac{1}{n}$; 4 in.
4. $\frac{2}{5} = \frac{n}{70}$; 28 in.
5. $\frac{27.5}{n} = \frac{1}{4}$; 110 m

Lesson 2.8, page 20

1. 440 inches
2. 8 inches
3. 4.5 centimeters
4. 36 feet
5. 12.5 feet
6. 8 inches

Lesson 2.8, page 21

1. 54 feet
2. 80 feet
3. 17 inches
4. 27 miles
5. 1 inch = $\frac{7}{4}$ feet
6. 1 inch = $\frac{4}{5}$ foot

Lesson 2.9, page 22

	a	b	c
1.	3	9	7
2.	2	10	12
3.	15	14	18

4. 2; 3; 3
5. 8; 9; 9
6. 11; 12; 12
7. 9; 10; 9
8. 15; 16; 16

Lesson 2.10, page 23

1. $\sqrt{74} = 8.60$
2. $\sqrt{100} = 10$
3. $\sqrt{97} = 9.85$
4. $\sqrt{34} = 5.83$
5. $\sqrt{40} = 6.32$
6. $\sqrt{117} = 10.82$
7. $\sqrt{80} = 8.94$
8. $\sqrt{25} = 5$
9. $\sqrt{85} = 9.22$
10. $\sqrt{106} = 10.30$

Lesson 2.11, page 24

1. $A = (a + b)^2$
2. $A = 0.5(\text{base})(\text{height}) = 0.5ab$
3. $4(0.5ab) = 2ab$
4. c^2
5. $2ab + c^2$
6. $(a + b)^2 = 2ab + c^2$; set the two areas equal
   $a^2 + 2ab + b^2 = 2ab + c^2$; multiply $(a + b)^2$
   $a^2 + b^2 = c^2$; subtract $2ab$ from both sides
7. $A = 0.5(a + b)(a + b)$
   $A = 0.5(a + b)^2$
8. $0.5ab + 0.5ab + 0.5c^2$
   $ab + 0.5c^2$
9. $0.5(a + b)^2 = ab + 0.5c^2$; set the two areas equal
   $0.5(a^2 + 2ab + b^2) = ab + 0.5c^2$; multiply $(a + b)^2$
   $a^2 + 2ab + b^2 = 2ab + c^2$; multiply by 2 on both sides
   $a^2 + b^2 = c^2$; subtract $2ab$ from both sides

Geometry Answers

Lesson 2.11, page 25
1. $a^2 + b^2 = d^2$
2. $a^2 + b^2 = c^2$
3. $c^2 = d^2$
4. $c = d$
5. Because they have the same side lengths.
6. The measure is 90°.
7. right triangle

Lesson 2.12, page 26
1. $\sqrt{36}$ or 6
2. $\sqrt{112}$ or 10.58
3. $\sqrt{160}$ or 12.65
4. $\sqrt{132}$ or 11.49
5. $\sqrt{48}$ or 6.93
6. $\sqrt{2,200} = 46.90$
7. $\sqrt{820} = 28.64$

Lesson 2.13, page 27
1. 21 feet
2. 9 miles
3. 8.66 feet
4. 65 feet
5. 15.3 km

Lesson 2.14, page 28
	a	b	c
1.	12.53	11.18	10.30
2.	14.32	12.17	12.37

Lesson 2.14, page 29
	a	b	c
1.	9.85	8.54	9.90
2.	9.06	6.40	6.71
3.	8.54	8.60	8.49

Check What You Learned, page 30
	a	b	c
1.	20°; obtuse	50°; acute	90°, 25°; right
2.	scalene	isosceles	equilateral
3.	$\frac{14}{84} = \frac{1}{6}$;	$\frac{32}{192} = \frac{1}{6}$;	$\frac{38}{228} = \frac{1}{6}$; similar

	a	b
4.	128 ft.	44 m

Check What You Learned, page 31
	a	b	c
5.	11	16	12
6.	9	10	9
7.	$\sqrt{1213}$; 34.83		
8.	$\sqrt{6160}$; 78.49		
9.	$\sqrt{19968}$; 141.31		
10.	39 feet		
11.	270 m	120 m	150 m

Chapter 3

Check What You Know, page 32
1a. decagon; 1440°; 144°
1b. quadrilateral; 360°; 90°
1c. hexagon; 720°; 120°
2a. heptagon; 900°; 128.57°
2b. octagon; 1080°; 135°
2c. pentagon; 540°; 108°
3a. rhombus; equilateral
3b. triangle; regular
3c. hexagon; equiangular

Lesson 3.1, page 33
1a. decagon; 1440°; 144°
1b. hexagon; 720°; 120°
1c. triangle; 180°; 60°
2a. quadrilateral; equilateral
2b. heptagon; regular
2c. quadrilateral; equiangular

Lesson 3.1, page 34
1a. A, C; A, D; B, D; B, E; C, E; convex

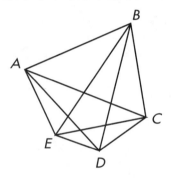

1b. F, H; F, I; G, I; G, J; H, J; concave

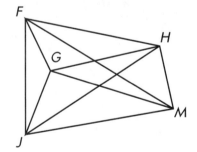

2a. K, M; L, N; convex

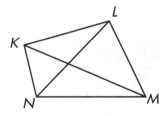

Geometry Answers

2b. W, Y; X, Z; convex

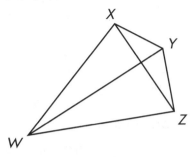

Lesson 3.2, page 35

1. square, rectangle, rhombus
2. rectangle, parallelogram
3. D has 4 congruent sides.
4. trapezoid
5. 65°
6. rhombus, parallelogram
7. 70°
8. kite

Lesson 3.3, page 36

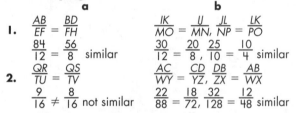

	a	b
1.	$\frac{AB}{EF} = \frac{BD}{FH}$	$\frac{IK}{MO} = \frac{IJ}{MN}, \frac{JL}{NP} = \frac{LK}{PO}$
	$\frac{84}{12} = \frac{56}{8}$ similar	$\frac{30}{12} = \frac{20}{8}, \frac{25}{10} = \frac{10}{4}$ similar
2.	$\frac{QR}{TU} = \frac{QS}{TV}$	$\frac{AC}{WY} = \frac{CD}{YZ}, \frac{DB}{ZX} = \frac{AB}{WX}$
	$\frac{9}{16} \neq \frac{8}{16}$ not similar	$\frac{22}{88} = \frac{18}{72}, \frac{32}{128} = \frac{12}{48}$ similar

Check What You Learned, page 37

1a. pentagon; 540°; 108°
1b. octagon; 1080°; 135°
1c. triangle; 180°; 60°
2a. quadrilateral; 360°; 90°
2b. nonagon; 1260°; 140°
2c. heptagon; 900°; 128.57°
3a. pentagon; equiangular
3b. hexagon; regular
3c. quadrilateral; equilateral

Check What You Learned, page 38

4. trapezoid; bases; legs
5. 360°; 70°
6. parallelogram; 128°
7. 90°
8. Figure D: A, C; B, D; Figure E: J, L; J, M; K, M; K, N; L, N
9. Figure E

	a	b
10.	$\frac{AB}{EF} = \frac{BD}{FH}, \frac{AC}{EG} = \frac{CD}{GH}$	$\frac{JK}{NO} = \frac{KM}{OQ}$
	$\frac{18}{12} = \frac{30}{20}$ similar	$\frac{30}{10} \neq \frac{20}{8}$ not similar

Mid-Test (Chapters 1–3), page 39

1. ray
2. ABE, GBC
3. acute
4. ∠CBE
5. ∠FBG
6. 45°
7. ∠ABG, ∠CBE
8. ∠3, ∠6; ∠4, ∠5
9. ∠1, ∠8; ∠2, ∠7
10. 110°
11. $\overleftrightarrow{NO}$
12. ∠1 or ∠4

Mid-Test (Chapters 1–3), page 40

13.–16. Use a protractor and ruler to check the accuracy of the drawings.

17. $\frac{\$14}{\text{pie}} = \frac{\$700}{n \text{ pies}}$; $\$14n = \$700$; $n = 50$
18. $\frac{2 \text{ cm}}{1 \text{ ft.}} = \frac{l \text{ cm}}{14 \text{ ft.}}$; $l = 28$ cm; $\frac{2 \text{ cm}}{1 \text{ ft.}} = \frac{w \text{ cm}}{12 \text{ ft.}}$; $w = 24$ cm

Mid-Test (Chapters 1–3), page 41

	a	b	c
19.	17°; obtuse	85°; acute	15°; 90°; right
	a	**b**	
20.	25 m	34 ft.	

21. parallelogram; opposite
22. parallel; kite
23. rectangle; parallelogram
24. square; congruent

Mid-Test (Chapters 1–3), page 42

25. $\frac{18}{25} = 0.72$ in.; $\frac{10}{12} = 0.83$ in.; $\frac{15}{22} = 0.68$ in.; not similar
26. $\sqrt{56} = 7.48$
27. $\sqrt{100} = 10$
28. $\sqrt{23,775} = 154.19$
29. mast^2 = 122 − 72; mast^2 = 144 − 49; mast = $\sqrt{95}$, or 9.75 ft.
30. 9.22
31. 7.62
32. 7.21

Geometry Answers

Chapter 4

Check What you Know, page 43

	a	b	c
1.	–16	0	–21
2.	6	5	–11
3.	14	–20	9
4.	7	–5	0

	a	b
5.	E	G
6.	D	B
7.	(2, 6)	(6, 5)
8.	(2, 2)	(4, 7)

9.–11.

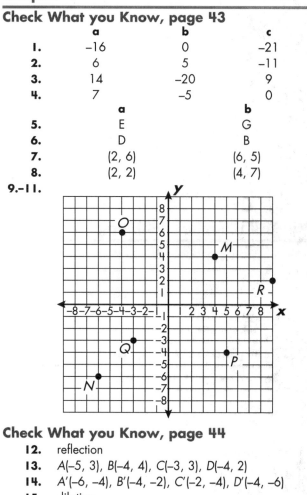

Check What you Know, page 44

12. reflection
13. A(–5, 3), B(–4, 4), C(–3, 3), D(–4, 2)
14. A'(–6, –4), B'(–4, –2), C'(–2, –4), D'(–4, –6)
15. dilation
16.

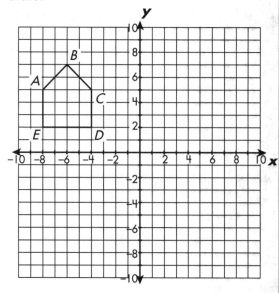

17. pentagon

Lesson 4.1, page 45

	a	b	c
1.	9	8	8
2.	–7	–9	12
3.	–35	–9	–20
4.	–12	–22	–11
5.	0	2	1
6.	–10	11	–19

Lesson 4.2, page 46

1. H, E
2. D, G
3. L(9, 5), C(3, 3)
4. J(1, 8), I(5, 3)
5. F(8, 8), K(7, 4)

6.–7.

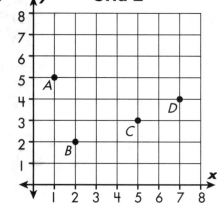

Grid 2

Lesson 4.2, page 47

1.–5.

Grid 1

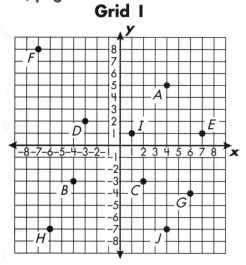

6. A(7, 6), B(–2, 5)
7. C(–3, –2), D(3, –3)
8. E(–4, 7), F(–4, –6)
9. G(5, 4), H(7, –4)
10. I(–8, –5), J(–6, 2)

Geometry Answers

Lesson 4.3, page 48
1a. dilation
1b. rotation
1c. translation or reflection
2a. rotation
2b. reflection
2c. dilation
3a. reflection or rotation
3b. translation or reflection
3c. translation

Lesson 4.4, page 49
	a	b	c
1.	yes	no	yes
2.	yes	no	no
3.	no	no	yes

Lesson 4.5, page 50
	a	b	c
1.	yes	yes	no
2.	no	yes	no
3.	no	yes	yes

Lesson 4.6, page 51
	a	b	c
1.	yes	no	no
2.	no	yes	yes
3.	yes	no	yes

Lesson 4.7, page 52
	a	b	c
1.	reflection	rotation	translation
2.	reflection	rotation	reflection
3.	translation	reflection	translation
4.	reflection	translation	rotation

Lesson 4.8, page 53
	a	b	c
1.	yes	yes	no
2.	no	yes	yes
3.	yes	no	yes

Lesson 4.9, page 54
	a	b	c
1.	translation, yes	translation, yes	reflection, yes
2.	reflection, yes	dilation, no	rotation, yes
3.	translation, yes	rotation, yes	dilation, no

Lesson 4.9, page 55
1. (–4, –1), (–1, –1), (–1, –4), (–2, –4)
2. (–4, 1), (–1, 1), (–1, 4), (–2, 4)
3. reflection
4. yes
5. (–5, 1), (–1, 1), (–1, 4)
6. (–2, –2), (2, –2), (2, 1)
7. translation
8. yes

Lesson 4.9, page 56
1. (–4, 3), (0, 3), (–2, 1), (–6, 1)
2.

3. dilation
4. (2, 3), (5, 1), (1, 0)
5.

6. rotation
7. (2,5), (0,0), (5,3), (5,1)
8.

9. reflection

Lesson 4.10, page 57
	a	b	c
1.	congruent	neither	neither
2.	neither	congruent	similar

Lesson 4.10, page 58
Answers will vary.
1a. rotate 90°; dilate by a factor of 2; translate +9 on the y-axis and –10 on the x-axis; similar
1b. reflect on the x-axis; translate +10 on the x-axis; congruent

Geometry Answers

Lesson 4.11, page 59

1. trapezoid

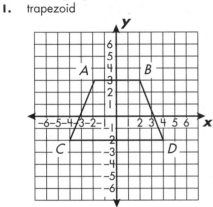

2. quadrilateral

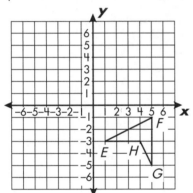

3. parallelogram

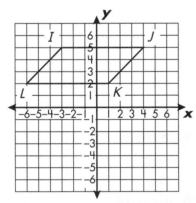

Check What You Learned, page 60

	a	b	c
1.	14	–3	–26
2.	–6	–4	–11
3.	15	17	–9
4.	–4	41	2

5. B, E
6. C, G
7. A(10, 5), H(7, 4)
8. F(4, 9), D(1,1)

9.–11.

Grid 1

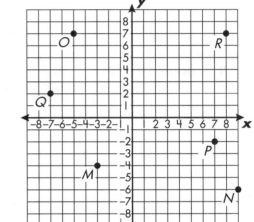

Check What You Learned, page 61

12. rotation
13. translation
14. A(1, –3), B(3, –1), C(6, –1), D(4, –3)
15. A'(–6, 2), B'(–4, 4), C'(–1, 4), D'(–3, 2)
16.

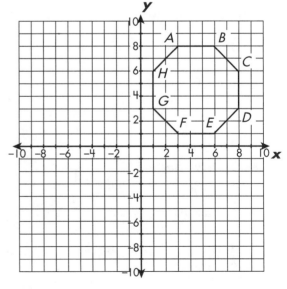

17. octagon

Geometry Answers

Chapter 5

Check What You Know, page 62

1. C
2. C
3. $\overline{CD}$, $\overline{CE}$, $\overline{CF}$
4. $\overline{EF}$, $\overline{GH}$
5. $\overline{EF}$
6. 87.92 in.; 75.36 cm; 106.76 yd.
7. E
8. G
9. B
10. F
11. C
12. D
13. A

Check What You Know, page 63

14. radius
15. origin
16. 5 ft.; 2.5 ft.
17. 37.68 ft.
18. cylinder
19. square

Lesson 5.1, page 64

	a	b	c
1.	radius	diameter	chord
2.	A		
3.	A		

4. $\overline{AB}$, $\overline{AC}$, $\overline{AD}$
5. $\overline{CD}$, $\overline{EF}$
6. $\overline{CD}$
7. Answers will vary. One possible answer is shown.

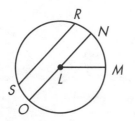

Lesson 5.2, page 65

	a	b	c
1.	3 ft.	1.5 ft.	9.42 ft.
2.	37 cm	18.5 cm	116.18 cm
3.	24 yd.	12 yd.	75.36 yd.
4.	4.5 mm	2.25 mm	14.13 mm
5.	10 km	5 km	31.4 km
6.	24.2 in.	12.1 in.	75.99 in.
7.	10.5 mi.	5.25 mi.	32.97 mi.
8.	1.5 cm	0.75 cm	4.71 cm
9.	9.6 ft.	4.8 ft.	30.14 ft.

Lesson 5.3, page 66

1. triangular pyramid
2. rectangular solid
3. cylinder
4. triangular solid
5. square pyramid
6. cone
7. 4 faces; triangular
8. 6 faces; rectangular
9. 2 faces; circular
10. 5 faces; 2 triangular, 3 rectangular
11. 5 faces; 1 square, 4 triangular
12. 1 face; circular

Lesson 5.4, page 67

1. Shaylin
2. diameter
3. 6 in.; 3 in.
4. 6.28 ft.
5. cube
6. cylinder

Check What You Learned, page 68

1. origin
2. diameter
3. radius
4. chord
5. A
6. 6 mi.; 226.08 ft.; 18 mm
7. D
8. E
9. G
10. A
11. F
12. C
13. B

Check What You Learned, page 69

14. diameter
15. $C = \pi \times d$ or $C = 2 \times \pi \times r$
16. 13.5 cm; 6.75 cm
17. 18.84 yd.
18. The square pyramid has 1 square base.
19. the intersection of 2 faces

Geometry Answers

Chapter 6

Check What You Know, page 70

	a	b	c
1.	45 in.	43 yd.	41 mm
2a.	$A = 165$ cm^2; $P = 52$ cm		
2b.	$l = 19$ ft.; $P = 64$ ft.		
2c.	$s = 9$ mm; $P = 36$ mm		
3.	85 in.^{2}	100 m^2	40.5 cm^2

Check What You Know, page 71

	a	b	c
4.	6 cm	12 cm	113.04 cm^2
5.	7.5 ft.	15 ft.	176.63 ft.^{2}
6.	5 in.	10 in.	78.5 in.^{2}
7.	1201.05 m^2	213.52 cm^2	108 yd.^{2}
8.	189 ft.^{2}	1299.96 mm^2	19.15 in.^{2}
9.	943 cm^2		
10.	7.07 yd.^{2}		

Lesson 6.1, page 72

	a	b	c
1.	$2\frac{1}{2}$ ft.	50 yd.	$7\frac{1}{4}$ in.
2.	$1\frac{4}{5}$ cm	16 ft.	19.2 cm
3.	14 in.	16 m	10 mi.

Lesson 6.2, page 73

	a	b	c
1.	8 m^2	36 mi.^{2}	128 ft.^{2}
2.	75 mm^2	144 in.^{2}	48 yd.^{2}
3.	15 ft.	2.2 m	11 cm

Lesson 6.3, page 74

	a	b	c
1.	168 yd.^{2}	59.5 cm^2	200 m^2
2.	100 m^2	103.95 mi.^{2}	375 ft.^{2}
3.	462 in.^{2}	128 mm^2	180 mm^2

Lesson 6.4, page 75

	a	b	c
1.	288 m^2	9 cm^2	87 yd.^{2}
2.	25 ft.^{2}	101 in.^{2}	67.5 m^2
3.	84 ft.^{2}	45 mm^2	19.25 in.^{2}

Lesson 6.5, page 76

	a	b	c
1.	8 mm	16 mm	200.96 mm^2
2.	6 ft.	12 ft.	113.04 ft.^{2}
3.	4 yd.	8 yd.	50.24 yd.^{2}
4.	9 cm	18 cm	254.34 cm^2
5.	2.5 mi.	5 mi.	19.63 mi.^{2}
6.	13 m	26 m	530.66 m^2
7.	3.5 mm	7 mm	38.47 mm^2
8.	5.75 in.	11.5 in.	103.82 in.^{2}
9.	21 ft.	42 ft.	1,384.74 ft.^{2}
10.	15 cm	30 cm	706.5 cm^2

Lesson 6.6, page 77

	a	b	c
1.	810 in.^{2}	160 yd.^{2}	198.75 ft.^{2}
2.	32 m^2	1,254 mm^2	832 m^2
3.	960 cm^2	60 in.^{2}	1,067.45 ft.^{2}

Lesson 6.7, page 78

	a	b	c
1.	21.52 cm^2	2,840 in.^{2}	217.26 ft.^{2}
2.	214 yd.^{2}	104 m^2	696 cm^2
3.	108 mm^2	203.26 ft.^{2}	1,548 in.^{2}

Lesson 6.8, page 79

1.	102 sq. in.	**3.**	480 sq. yd.	**5.**	375 sq. in.
2.	788 sq. in.	**4.**	72 sq. in.	**6.**	3,600 sq. yd.

Lesson 6.8, page 80

1.	500 sq. m	**3.**	146 cm	**5.**	1,340 sq. cm
2.	1.43 sq. m	**4.**	87.72 sq. m	**6.**	168 sq. cm

Lesson 6.9, page 81

	a	b	c
1.	502.4 ft.^{2}	75.36 cm^2	2,090.49 m^2
2.	1,531.32 mm^2	1,139.82 yd.^{2}	485.07 cm^2
3.	235.5 mm^2	7,834.43 in.^{2}	505.54 ft.^{2}

Lesson 6.10, page 82

	a	b	c
1.	100.48 in.^{2}	502.4 mm^2	381.51 ft.^{2}
2.	615.44 cm^2	1758.4 in.^{2}	244.92 yd.^{2}
3.	1,295.25 m^2	2,122.64 ft.^{2}	879.2 m^2

Lesson 6.11, page 83

1.

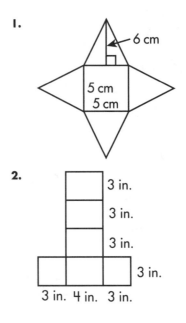

2.

Geometry Answers

3.

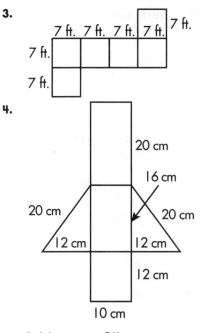

4.

Lesson 6.11, page 84

1. 224 in.²;

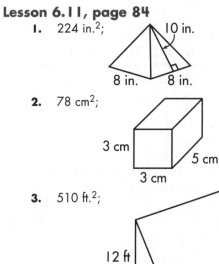

2. 78 cm²;

3. 510 ft.²;

4. 96 yd²;

5. 96 cm²;

Lesson 6.12, page 85

	a	b
1.	rectangle	rectangle
2.	quadrilateral	quadrilateral
3.	rectangle	rectangle

Lesson 6.12, page 86

	a	b
1.	triangle	trapezoid
2.	square	triangle
3.	triangle	trapezoid

Lesson 6.13, page 87

1. 250 ft.; 3750 ft.²
2. 484 ft.²
3. 80 in.²; 8 in.
4. 76.5 ft.²
5. 2 m; 3.14 m²

Check What You Learned, page 88

	a	b	c
1.	24 cm	16 m	28 in.
2a.	$s = 14$ m; $P = 56$ m		
2b.	$A = 41.25$ yd.²; $P = 26$ yd.		
2c.	$A = 323$ mm²; $P = 96$ mm		
3.	272 ft.²	404 cm²	29.25 yd.²
4.	3.5 yd.	7 yd.	38.47 yd.²
5.	8 m	16 m	201 m²

Check What You Learned, page 89

	a	b	c
6.	560 m²	1,758.4 cm²	200.96 ft.²
7.	95.71 in.²	85 m²	79.68 mm²
8.	6,000 ft.; 18,000 ft.		
9.	339.12 in.²; 904.32 in.²; 1,243.44 in.²		

Chapter 7

Check What You Know, page 90

	a	b	c
1.	5,184 in.³	8 ft.³	32,000 mm³
2.	6 yd.³	4,000 cm³	343 m³
3.	226.08 ft.³	1,356.48 cm³	34,335.9 mm³
4.	75.36 in.³	150.72 ft.³	410.29 cm³

Check What You Know, page 91

	a	b	c
5.	3.33 yd.³	16.77 in.³	5,760 cm³
6.	2,356 cm³		
7.	720 in.³		
8.	16.49 in.³		

Lesson 7.1, page 92

	a	b	c
1.	2,240 cm³	6 m³	108 in.³
2.	450 cm³	150 ft.³	487,500 mm³
3.	64 cm³	72 ft.³	60 in.³

Geometry Answers

Lesson 7.2, page 93

	a	b
1.	$\frac{30}{343}$ cu. in.	$\frac{4}{243}$ cu. ft.
2.	$\frac{160}{729}$ cu. cm	$\frac{40}{1331}$ cu. ft.

Lesson 7.3, page 94

	a	b	c
1.	12 ft.^{3}	121 in.^{3}	24 m^3
2.	96 yd.^{3}	110.25 in.^{3}	4.5 m^3
3.	80 ft.^{3}	84 cm^3	324,000 mm^3

Lesson 7.4, page 95

	a	b	c
1.	13,423.5 cm^3	211.95 ft.^{3}	34,710.35 in.^{3}
2.	4,747.68 mm^3	7,269.89 in.^{3}	271,296 cm^3
3.	16,786.44 m^3	301.44 ft.^{3}	95.39 yd.^{3}

Lesson 7.5, page 96

	a	b	c
1.	102.57 ft.^{3}	942 m^3	1,130.4 in.^{3}
2.	588.75 cm^3	158.96 ft.^{3}	1,808.64 in.^{3}
3.	8,138.88 ft.^{3}	2,077.11 cm^3	301.44 m^3

Lesson 7.6, page 97

	a	b	c
1.	1,176 cm^3	11,200 in.^{3}	1,109.33 ft.^{3}
2.	3,072 m^3	3,200 mm^3	416.67 cm^3
3.	2,000 mm^3	75 m^3	972 ft.^{3}

Lesson 7.7, page 98

	a	b	c
1.	2,143.57 in.^{3}	523.33 km^3	4,186.67 m^3
2.	904.32 ft.^{3}	1,436.03 cm^3	113.04 in.^{3}
3.	4,186.67 cm^3	904.32 yd.^{3}	267.95 ft.^{3}

Lesson 7.8, page 99

1. 508.68 cubic inches
2. 6,430.72 cubic centimeters
3. B; 116.18 cubic centimeters
4. 1,334.5 cubic centimeters
5. 14.13 cubic inches
6. 523.33 cubic inches

Lesson 7.9, page 100

1. 1,153.95 cm^3
2. 24 in.^{3}
3. 29.44 in.^{3}
4. 56.52 cm^3 for each cupcake; 678.24 cm^3 for 12 cupcakes

Check What You Learned, page 101

	a	b	c
1.	1,130.4 cm^3	33.51 mi.^{3}	9,495.36 yd.^{3}
2.	10,368 mm^3	502.4 ft.^{3}	37.68 m^3
3.	4.71 m^3	972 cm^3	6,000 in.^{3}
4.	523.33 cm^3	2,688 cm^3	1,570 ft.^{3}

Check What You Learned, page 102

	a	b	c
5.	1,706.67 in.^{3}	1.76 m^3	7,476 in.^{3}

6. 40.21 in.^{3} for one jar; 241.26 in.^{3} for six jars
7. 131.25 cm^3 for one serving; 1,968.75 cm^3 for fifteen servings
8. 5,832 in.^{3}

Final Test (Chapters 1–7), page 103

1. $\angle JIB$
2. obtuse
3. $\angle HIG$
4. $\overleftrightarrow{GD}$
5. $\angle IJC$
6. $\frac{1 \text{ cm}}{1.25 \text{ mi.}} = \frac{12 \text{ cm}}{x \text{ mi.}}$; $x = 15$ miles
7. $\frac{3 \text{ rabbits}}{2 \text{ goats}} = \frac{18 \text{ rabbits}}{y \text{ goats}}$; $y = 12$ goats
8. $\frac{AB}{DE} = \frac{34}{51} = \frac{2}{3}$; $\frac{BC}{EF} = \frac{28}{42} = \frac{2}{3}$; $\frac{CB}{DF} = \frac{48}{72} = \frac{2}{3}$; similar

	a	b
9.	25 m	34 ft.

Final Test (Chapters 1–7), page 104

10. $n = (180 - n) - 65$; 57.5 degrees; 122.5 degrees

	a	b
11.	6.24 in.	15 in.

12. 360°; equiangular
13. convex
14. trapezoid; rhombus; A trapezoid has only one pair of parallel sides while a rhombus has two.
15. 720°; 120°

Geometry Answers

Final Test (Chapters 1–7), page 105

16. 20 ft.

17.

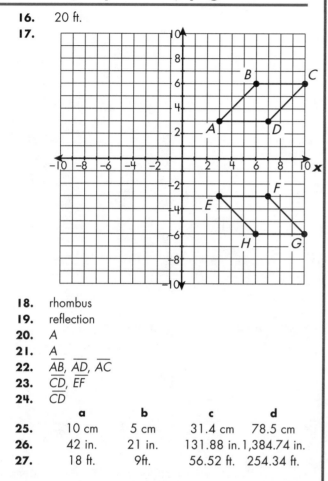

18. rhombus

19. reflection

20. A

21. A

22. $\overline{AB}$, $\overline{AD}$, $\overline{AC}$

23. $\overline{CD}$, $\overline{EF}$

24. $\overline{CD}$

	a	b	c	d
25.	10 cm	5 cm	31.4 cm	78.5 cm
26.	42 in.	21 in.	131.88 in.	1,384.74 in.
27.	18 ft.	9ft.	56.52 ft.	254.34 ft.

Final Test (Chapters 1–7), page 106

28a.	$P = 92$ cm	$A = 529$ cm^2
28b.	$P = 36$ mm	$A = 93.6$ mm^2
28c.	$P = 44.14$ in.	$A = 67.5$ in.^{2}
29a.	$P = 37.4$ in.	$A = 70$ in.^{2}
29b.	$SA = 768$ mm^2	$V = 1,152$ mm^3
29c.	$SA = 864$ cm^2	$V = 1,296$ cm^3
30a.	$SA = 1,099$ cm^2	$V = 2,769.48$ cm^3
30b.	$SA = 885.6$ ft.^{2}	$V = 972$ ft.^{3}
30c.	$SA = 240.21$ ft.^{2}	$V = 235.5$ ft.^{3}

Notes

Notes

Notes